The Game Conservatory

01425-652381

Wild Partridge Management — 8.95
Game in Winter Feeding & Management — 10.50
Predator Control. — 10.50

Your Shoot — Ian McCall — Black
The Amateur Keeper — Archie Coates.

Supplied by
TIDELINE BOOKS
49 Kinmel Street
Rhyl. Clwyd
North Wales LL18 1AG
Tel 01745 354919

PARTRIDGE FOR SPORT

PARTRIDGE FOR SPORT

Geoffrey Nightingale

Sketches and Illustrations   Felicity Nightingale
Photographs   Paul Middleton and Others

THE BOYDELL PRESS

© Geoffrey Nightingale 1990

All Rights Reserved. Except as permitted under current legislation no part of this work may be photocopied, stored in a retrieval system, published, performed in public, adapted, broadcast, transmitted, recorded or reproduced in any form or by any means, without the prior permission of the copyright owner

First published 1990 by The Boydell Press, Woodbridge

The Boydell Press is an imprint of Boydell & Brewer Ltd
PO Box 9, Woodbridge, Suffolk IP12 3DF

ISBN 0 85115 256 2

British Library Cataloguing in Publication Data
Nightingale, Geoffrey
 Partridge for sport.
 1. Livestock: Partridges
 I. Title
 636.59
 ISBN 0–85115–256–2

This publication is printed on acid-free paper

Printed and bound in Great Britain by
Southampton Book Company Ltd, Southampton, Hants

CONTENTS

Acknowledgements	vii
Introduction	1
The Partridge	7
The Stock	22
Red-legs or Greys	27
The Pens	30
Siting the Pens	38
Feeding	48
The Release	63
Driving Partridge	67
The Second Syndicate	80
Of Dogs and Pickers-up	85
Keepers and Beaters	91
Timing	98
Vermin	107
Rats, Rats and Rats	111
Cave Canem	120
Foxes	125
The Working Party	130
Postscript	135
Conclusion	145
Bibliography	150
Appendix	151

ACKNOWLEDGEMENTS

The Author acknowledges the permission kindly given to quote from the following works: Howard & Moore, *A Complete Checklist of the Birds of the World* (1980), by permission of the Oxford University Press; Brian Vesey-FitzGerald, *British Game* (1946), Collins, St James Place London, by permission of the estate of the late Brian Vesey-FitzGerald.

He also wishes to thank Garry Owen, who inspired and was the template for this book, and all those who spelt, illustrated, puzzled, photographed, typed and suggested without expectation of reward or hope of publication.

A great wild country

INTRODUCTION

> Ours is a great wild country,
> If you climb to our castle's top.
> I don't see where your eye can stop;
> *The Flight of the Duchess*, Robert Browning

Not quite what Browning was describing, but a rolling downland interlaced with roads and rights of way and infested with dog walkers – I am one of them myself. A pastoral scene of great charm and sterility where roadside flowers flourish the whole year round: plastic cups, tin cans and spare shoes, occasionally that harbinger of Spring, a woollen garment hanging from a blackthorn bush. Farming here is carried on by the modern method, that is to say, animate objects are regularly milked and anything inanimate is ploughed or cut. Those mischievous gifts of a cynical providence, the hedgecutter and the bulldozer, are much in evidence. Farmers with a taste for conservation leave the old barbed wire in the hedgerows as they strain the new. Many who farm in this way, that is to say efficiently, go out of their way to plant small woods on these inhospitable downs; to make a pond or to leave the occasional area of planned neglect. Who are we to criticise who would ourselves operate in exactly the same way were we to have the task of making a living from the land. I used to say that it was worth a thousand a year to work in this locality but inflation has out-dated that expression and left me bereft of words. Perhaps I was right when, as I stood on a hill overlooking the blue sea at the start of a pheasant drive the other day, the thought occurred to me that the proper comparison would be the exchange of a working lifetime in the city for a few years of retirement here. The paths of some are set in pleasant places!

It is interesting to read of the proposals to curb overproduction; sad too, because all sportsmen are tied to the land and the prosperity of the farmer is the prosperity of us all. Among other things, I see that leaving twenty per cent of the land fallow has been advocated. Should that come about, I should have thought it would do more good for partridge than anything else is likely to do. The Game Conservancy are not so

The head keeper. *Paul Middleton*

sure: the history of the partridge is the history of success and failure. There were the early days when Gilbert White complained of selfish sportsmen making a bag of twenty or so in a day and the days when the partridge was the rough shooter's friend: always there, always coming back. Between times there were the years of abundance and those of scarcity: there were the eight year cycles, the curse of more and more land left in grass, the benefit of the plough when it came into fashion and the disadvantage of it when it was used too soon after harvest. The shepherd tells a tale of some years back when he saw two or three poachers on the hill and gave chase from the valley below. Despite their head start, he jumped the final wall to race down and catch the last of the poachers as he missed the pedal on attempting to mount his bike. The last wall the shepherd jumped led down to the valley by the road: steep sided with a bottom now thick with sheep or tenanted by store cattle where the Guns line up for the first drive. 'Of course,' he said, 'When I jumped that wall, it surprised the people there because there were four or five families picnicking. They used to come out from the town and picnic there regularly. It wasn't fenced off then and Peter's father never grazed it.' The shepherd is not an old man and one is not going back far to the days when this was a well known partridge manor.

What a land of milk and honey it must have been for the sportsman who never knew the need to put down birds: springing turf, harebells, scotch thistle, bramble and the odd gorse, rabbit scratchings and nettle patch, fields of stubble with wide headlands.

Our own farm, the centre of our Shoot, is very involved in our operations and a large area of stubble is left until after Christmas helped along by mustard which we are allowed to sow among the barley. In addition, generous headlands help a good deal in an inhospitable countryside. This year, we shall have an acre of kale in a broad strip running along our best flushing point and another acre at a further chosen point. We are in the position of being able to make the best of what we have and perhaps it is these more positive aspects I should be emphasising. We are all members of the same community, endeavouring to make the countryside fruitful, although our individual aims may diverge. That we are in the same boat is borne out by the description my head keeper gave me of the duck pond he hoped to have built. When it was finished, he said, he would surround the lot with a really good barbed wire fence! I wonder if there will be soft drink cans and empty cartridge cases there as well?

And I? Where do I fit in with all this? I am a sort of ugly duckling, the odd one out, as evinced by the fact that I am the vermin man as well as honorary legal advisor to the Shoot! I might well be scorned or even barred from the Shoot as a man with rabbiting dogs, but I have an inestimable advantage over all the young fit bodies on the Shoot: I am a retired person. It is in these circumstances as a general odd job man that I ask my head keeper how I am to keep the pens from flooding, what book shall I read to learn about straying partridge, why the birds are not in the rape today and where shall I get the low-down on foxes? I might as well be a carpenter addressing an oyster, for answer comes there none! There seems to be no book on the partridge that deals adequately with these questions or the many others that come to one's mind: nor can I purport to write one. I can, however, raise the questions and describe my own experiences and repeat a good deal of the lore fed to me by my head keeper. There must be many gaps when a man such as I writes a book; it is no good my dealing with things that I have not seen and experienced and there are many things that I have allowed to pass unnoticed. This is just a story about a small Shoot. Those who want to try downland partridge may find something useful here – I hope they do, but they must appreciate the limitations. They must start by reading the Game Conservancy booklets Nos 4 and 18 and treat this book as a dessert, although as such it is one that could well upset the knowledgeable stomach.

I also write because I always suspect that knowledgeable authors overestimate my ability to grasp a subject, and perhaps the ability of other beginners, and I have wondered if it might not be better to write about a subject before one's own knowledge and experience have obscured the simpler elements of it. I know that I seek charity in doing so, but perhaps the rather exhausting story of my struggle with rats, my joustings with foxes and other matters, will give confidence to some – while other readers may appreciate our efforts on the Shoot to provide suitable pens and feeders and set their own minds to work.

It is right that at some stage I should say something about my head keeper, and the first thing I should say is that every bit of technical information in this book which is correct came from him, and I'm not at all sure that I should absolve him from responsibility for the rest. Just as I have acknowledged that all that is good has come from him, so I might say that such insularity of opinion as may be expressed here may be due to our combined lack of experience of the great number of Shoots one would have to study in order to set oneself up as an expert. Pheasants, yes; partridge, no. There are not so many partridge Shoots, there is not so much talk about partridge, not so many articles. So I may apologise for that, though I do not apologise for the novice nature of these notes.

This is, therefore, the story of our own Shoot, as told by the vermin man and, indeed, one who has difficulty in distinguishing a weasel from a stoat!

My head keeper is not a head keeper at all: I must make that clear. It embarrasses him to be called that, and he would alter it if he could, but, as he cannot, he accepts it as the inescapable eccentricity of a man who is available to do a lot of odd jobs and thus an important cog in the Shoot. He (it probably upsets him still more to be called 'my' head keeper) is a man of passion as far as partridge are concerned. A futile passion, indulged in the face of much opposition I sometimes think, but one which has ruled his life for many years. Consequently, he knows a great deal that I do not necessarily extract from him and as I make clear, I am but an amanuensis as far as this book is concerned. It may be that I call him a head keeper as a sort of exaggeration of my own role from which I derive a great deal of amusement.

Indeed, the head keeper is only a spare time man, an amateur as we all are on this Shoot. In his limited spare time, he is concerned with more than one Shoot and more than one sporting activity. He uses his labour recklessly in the cause. As with any good keeper, his resting hours are devoted to planning the next move and pens put up on one day are often removed the next. Not a very good example of a planned move perhaps, but you will catch my gist. He spends much time and thought on his beaters who, for him, are the stuff of life. In physical labours he seems untiring: whether it be the early walk round before a shooting day starts or in the arduous labour of levelling a site. Tools (generally borrowed) are broken and thrust aside. He is not the sort of person to whom one should ever lend a knife! Fortunately, he bears criticism well and will accept any good advice. Since he is a mere amateur, he is a nobody in the keepering world.

We think we have achieved improvements in our methods of penning the birds and in our methods of release and it is these improvements, as we think them to be, that have led to this book being written. We hope that it will light up areas for investigation, lead to some questions being answered and emphasise the value that may be put on a few broad acres that are today empty of game and virtually free for the taking to be built up, by sweat and labour, into a modest partridge Shoot. The partridge is not an unintelligent bird and no doubt feels a little awkward when released into our present environment. He is a very charming bird, whether showing as a covey of twenty Red-legs running along the plough ahead, or exploding, as will a covey of Greys, up and up and along with the wind, listening to none of the shot passing behind. The partridge represents a challenge it is difficult to ignore. I do not mean the challenge to the Gun, but a challenge to the person who would show it to the Gun, and to the gamekeeper who is beset with unsuitable cultivations, with predators with two legs and with four, mischievous human, mammal and bird of prey, everything that eats meat, then add kind hearted vegetarian and loving dog owner. Only the fish seem neutral and, looking at the gloomy skies of this particular season, one wonders how long fish will be able to stay out of the game.

THE PARTRIDGE

> I like the pheasants and feeding things
>   Of the unsuspicious morn;
> I like the flap of the wood-pigeon's wings
>   As she rises from the corn.
> I like the blackbird's shriek and his rush
>   From the turnips as I pass by,
> And the partridge hiding her head in a bush,
>   For her young ones cannot fly.
> I like these things, and I like to ride
>   When all the world is in bed,
> To the top of the hill where the sky grows wide,
>   And where the sun grows red.
>   *The Old Squire*, Wilfred Scawen Blunt

A book on partridge would scarcely be complete without some description of the bird itself. There is always a danger that the novice may find himself beset by a covey of wild partridge whilst walking unknown ground and not be aware of the honour that is done him. More likely, a few facts here may save research elsewhere: but if the reader is intent on covering his subject thoroughly, then I recommend that he read *British Game* by Brian Vesey-FitzGerald and he will find in the section on partridge an excellent dissertation on the bird in which a close personal experience is wedded to the essential technical detail. Dr R. G. Potts' book, *The Partridge – Pesticides, Predation and Conservation*, is accurate, exciting and innovative. I should not call it a book: it is a monograph without any extraneous nonsense. Still, it is a very good book to have on your shelf. Mr Vesey-FitzGerald's book was published in 1946, so he may be classed as one of the old masters and it is my experience that, with the exception of Dr Potts' work, and such books as deal with rearing, that which the old experts do not tell you, you cannot expect to learn from a modern writer.

   Quite recently, a book was published which talks of the partridge as the bird which is likely to form the young man's introduction to shooting, and the bird from which the gun dog will learn his first lessons. Let

The Red-leg

me make it clear straight away that in the part of the world from which I come, the partridge is considered by shooting men to be an endangered species. Its existence here, I consider, is largely due to the fact that large numbers are released to give an early start to the shooting season, thus providing a resident population which even then only amounts to what would be considered a minimal breeding population in the more favoured parts of the country. That unseasonal start, if you like, makes partridge shooting here at once an expensive and sought after sport. We rely on reared birds and we cannot pen these, prior to release, before the harvest is over. Moreover, we have to order in advance, giving a delivery time when we are sure that the last of the harvest will have been gathered. Consequently there is no question of our shooting before October when the school holidays are well past. Not many schoolboys will join the ranks of our partridge shooters, and not many dogs will receive post graduate training in our partridge fields. I cannot believe that the partridge is so plentiful elsewhere, but if the remarks I have mentioned are translated into the context of a book written fifty years ago, then they make sense.

THE GREY AND THE RED-LEG

We are concerned in this country with two species of partridge. The Grey partridge, beloved of sportsmen and naturalists from time immemorial, is indigenous to this country, to Scotland and to Eire, in which latter country it thrives less well. The Red-leg was introduced from the continent in the eighteenth century and because of its irritating habit of running rather than rising to the Gun when walked up became known around the time of the Napoleonic wars as the 'Frenchman' or the 'French' partridge. Just over two hundred years later the first thing one says about the Red-leg is that it is a damned foreigner!

The prejudice against the running bird was so strong that it was regarded as more of a pest than as game and indeed was thought to drive the English Grey from the estate. A little more than one hundred years after their introduction so little had the Red-leg become accepted that Marksman wrote in his book *The Dead Shot*:

> At the present day they are looked upon by almost every sportsman as a nuisance, and the flavour of their flesh, as very far inferior to that of the English partridge. They never lie well; but baffle both the cunning of the dogs and the skill of the sportsman, especially any one unaccustomed to their habits.
>
> . . .
>
> The sportsman always rejoices at the victory which a heavy fall of snow enables him to make over these troublesome birds.
> He should take care to be out on an expedition of this kind as early in the morning as possible; and the birds are sure to be found in the fences. If he is desirous of exterminating the race of French partridges on his estate, a week's continuance of deep snows will afford him every opportunity of so doing: the previously wild and unapproachable species can be approached as they skulk in the fences, and driven out at his feet. They are thus entirely at his mercy, if he be only a tolerable shot. They are deprived of the very secret of their cunning and means of evasion, which lies entirely in their legs.

The Red-leg, as I shall call it, quickly settled down in this country proving itself as good a breeder, or better than, the Grey. In order to provide stock for release the Red-leg is now generally crossed with the Chukar, as to which more anon. This provides a slightly heavier bird that does well in captivity, lays well and is not given to feather pecking. The resultant cross is probably not a good breeder in the wild as yet and the EEC has regulations, yet to come into force as far as this bird is concerned, designed to prevent the release of alien species which may supplant the indigenous. I wonder if we would have been better off without the Red-leg? The Red-leg and the cross are heavier birds than is

The Grey

the Grey: less wild, more inclined to fly singly or in pairs and although an insect diet is most important for the survival of both species in their first three weeks of life the Red-leg chick is possibly capable of supporting itself rather better on a vegetable diet. The Red-leg is a splendid bird to release for driving.

THE FLIGHT, THE COVEY: PACKING

It is said that the partridge is the slowest flying of the game birds and it gives me great pleasure to emphasise that simple fact. It is enough to make you break your gun across your knee, is it not? As you know, the sudden uprush of birds if you are walking them up or the appearance of the covey over the hedge if you are a standing Gun is generally too much for one to cope with. One fails to pick one's bird and follow through, wait to see it fall before picking the second – I beg your pardon! I refer to my own inadequacies as though they were general! On the hills the partridge tends to fly rather faster than when he has merely to flip over a hedge to be (as it appears to him) out of sight. The Red-leg is the easier to shoot and this is not because he is any slower than the Grey though I think he might be but because he is the more likely to fly alone. His covey is quickly scattered and lacks the finer communication of the Grey. Just as they tend to scatter from their covey formation, although this is not an absolute rule, so will the Red-legs tend to pack so that you may have a bunch of fifty rising in front of you late in the season. It is sometimes necessary to return the birds over the Guns to break up the packs.

DISTINGUISHING MARKS, RED-LEGS AND GREYS: SEXING

Once seen at close quarters the Red-leg is easy to recognise again. Those which we release are always much tamer than the Greys and are more like young chicken as they make their way from you stretching out their necks. They achieve a fine barred flank, white throat with a dark jersey top becoming speckled at the chest. Red legs and beak complete the very colourful dress. Red-legs acquire their sartorial elegance at about eight to ten weeks of age. Easily distinguishable in captivity by the game farmer young Red-legs and young Greys are much the same in the field. A young covey of wild Red-legs will explode against the sky just as a covey of Greys will and unless you have seen the parents you will find it difficult to identify them. When the birds are young the parents of Red-legs and Greys give you every opportunity to identify them, running along in front of you, laying a false trail or affecting an injured wing. Otherwise the expert may be able to make a calculated guess as to the species from the position of the birds – whether they squat as the Greys are inclined to or run. When a new beater joins our line he will sometimes have occasion to point out a group of birds to the head keeper. The latter at once asks him are they Red-legs or Greys, putting the question in a manner that brooks no equivocation. 'Greys' comes the anxious reply. 'That's a funny place to see Greys', says my head keeper, 'Are you sure?' – 'No, Red-legs, I think,' says the unhappy beater. The keeper is content with this, he knows that the two types of bird are indistinguishable at that distance but he likes his little joke.

The Grey is the smaller bird and as the wild Grey comes out of the swedes to the side of the pen, desperately afraid of you but intrigued beyond caution by the new arrivals, there is something very attractive about him. One could never think of chicken in the same context. The two callers later left in the pen are an interesting study: this is the cock with the horseshoe of dark chestnut on the lower breast and the hen also with a horseshoe which, less distinct than that of the cock might be difficult to rely on were the two of them not side by side. Incidentally the best way to check the horseshoe is to first wring the bird's neck: at liberty the birds tend to keep low to the ground and the horseshoe is difficult to see. A more certain difference between the sexes lies in the faint crosslines on the hen's wing. The cock has no such transverse lines only the downward white stripes. The cock tends to a buff background here as against the darker background of the hen.

Sexing the Red-leg presents more of a problem to the keen student, less of a problem to me. Knobs, protuberances or embryo spurs on the tarsus (shank) of the cock can provide the answer if they are present. For separating the sexes the Game Conservancy recommend weighing each bird. Those exceeding 17½oz (500 gm) are likely to be cocks. When we leave callers in the pens we try to leave cocks or mostly cocks. We do this on the supposition that cocks have the greatest calling power. We seem to have no evidence to this effect but we feel that in any case the male bird, left out of the party, is likely to complain louder than the hen even if not lovingly. To this end we choose the larger birds and one gets to recognise the heavier bird and something slightly more aggressive in the bearing perhaps that denotes the cock. At any rate no one is likely to weigh or examine closely the birds which I have selected and that is why I choose my Red-leg cocks with a light heart, no book of reference in my hand. My word is law here and as I have said, sexing the Red-leg is a small problem to me.

AGE OF BIRDS

If you ask the keeper he should be able to tell you the age of the bird to the nearest day – unless it is a wild one! The old books recommend thinning out the senior birds severely each season leaving a vigorous young stock. How this is to be accomplished by the average shot they do not say but we must be careful in our criticism because the Guns in the days of plenty were used to shooting many more birds than we shoot today and with the sort of experience that they had no doubt came expertise. That useful little book *The Dead Shot* from which I have already quoted tells you how to come to terms with the partridge and in such a way as to create the impression that it was not unusual to mark down a covey and milk it of its members week by week. In such circumstances and following Marksman's advice one would no doubt attain an intimate knowledge of each member of the covey. Among the essays written in the *Spectator* and now known as the Coverly Papers is one written in 1710 where the shooting exploits of Sir Roger de Coverly are referred to: 'He has in his youthful days taken forty coveys of partridges in a season'. Again one gets the impression of a close acquaintance with the covey – over close perhaps – but certainly one where old and young could well be distinguished. Is there anything in the suggestion that when a covey is walked up the parents or older birds are the first to rise? Perhaps there is need for you when you are going through the birds after a shoot to distinguish the occasional second year bird. There were three old birds at the top of Caius wood last year and we never came up with them so we presumed that they had joined with a covey or more likely fallen prey to vermin. When the corn was cut in the same field this year I was surprised to see three adult birds who flew quickly, and I thought confidently, to cover as I stopped the car. They would be in their third year now and I expect they will need a bit of cooking if they ever take the wrong road on a shooting day. So how do you tell the age of a partridge? I think it is rather like sexing a Red-leg: a firm conviction that you are right will take you most of the way. With Greys the two outer primaries have pointed tips in first season birds and in the second season these become rounded. With Red-legs you wil find on the pure bred a narrow line of white at the tip and edge of the two outer primaries. This denotes the young bird as may a soft beak in the hands of a fancier. For research purposes the Game Conservancy give details of a test for age which involves checking the length of the bursa, a small blind passage on the upper side of the vent. Perhaps when our keepers have achieved a ninety per cent success in picking out undamaged birds for the Guns and the favoured few, we can proceed to a guarantee of tenderness also. For the moment I think myself that the one is as chancy as the other.

FOOD

The adult partridge is something of a vegetarian. No doubt this is so by necessity rather than by choice. It is recognised that the chicks need insect life in the first few weeks but after that they feed largely on weed seed or vegetable matter generally. Reared birds thrive on the pellets provided for their age group. They live well enough on wheat and less happily on barley (the two should not be mixed in the hoppers or the birds will peck out all the grain in search of that which they prefer). Where wheat is provided, I never seem to see a great deal of it in the crops of shot birds: one gets the feeling that the birds look to it for sustenance rather than relish. I may be too used to handling pheasants which enjoy the coarser fare so much more. At the same time the birds which are shot are plump enough and the birds one sees in early Spring seem bright and well fed. It is doubtful whether a lack of natural food is cause for partridge decline as far as the adult bird is concerned, although the lack of aphids and a shortage of insects may well account for the modest broods of most of those who do manage to rear. Those who read Dr Potts' monograph on partridge will be left in little doubt that modern spraying practice gives rise to a lack of insect food and in turn to starved chicks and the present decline. One of the most pleasant sights and one that comes to mind whenever I see the sprayer enter the field is that of Mrs Mother Hen when she is released with her brood in the morning. Off she takes them, whether they be a little group of pheasant chicks or her own young and this enormous parent teaches them to sip the dew from each blade of grass. As it turns out it is an unfortunate lesson for those young birds: indeed, a bad thing for any bird of the field to do. It is true of course that there are large areas of roughland subject to no sprays where you would expect a covey of Greys to live but which are as bare as can be. These areas are possibly more subject to predation but I suppose it is chiefly the honey pot of plough, corn and stubble that draws those coveys away, long enough at any rate for them to be affected to the same extent as any covey domiciled in the arable is affected by local conditions. The inquiring reader may like to refer to an excellent study, *Farming and Birds*, by R. J. O'Connor and Michael Shrubb (1986) and in particular the chapter on pesticides and pollution. It does seem from that that the marked decline in the sparrow hawk in the well wooded area of West Sussex between 1957 and 1963 might be explained by the westward drift of DDT from the orchards of Kent and East Sussex. Although one draws one's breath in at such a suggestion it must be remembered that a bird of prey would suffer the effects of a noxious spray through digesting birds more immediately subjected to it. The use of pesticides and their effect is now monitored by the Government.

PLUMAGE

I imagine that the partridge will soon conform to a British standards specification. I know that there are estates which still shoot wild birds year after year and skilfully maintain their stock, introducing no other. I cannot help feeling that there must be very few such estates. Over the country as a whole there are fewer wild birds and certainly many of the wild birds around here are released birds in their second year or the young of released birds. Thousands, perhaps millions, of partridges are released. Generally speaking these released birds are the product of birds raised in captivity from generation to generation. Will a standard bird result?

These reflections arise from a study of the older writers and their accounts of the distinguishing marks of the partridge. Brian Vesey-FitzGerald writes of the Grey in *British Game*:

> Many variations in colour occur, the most striking of which is that of the so called 'mountain', 'hill' and 'fell' partridge. In this the head and neck are a bright reddish-buff and most of the rest of the plumage is a rich chestnut red. The bird, in fact, looks not unlike a small grouse in the distance. In this variety the sexes are indistinguishable. Another variety is grey, shading off into pale yellow. In this the wing coverts of the bird are almost invariably barred with black. I have more than once seen albino partridges, and once shot a cock whose horseshoe was deep black.

It is pleasant to think of the harsh winds of the north or the fresh colours of the south imprinting their own distinction on the birds although one knows that through the years birds have been introduced from here, there and everywhere. Equally appealing must be the knowledge that this darker colour or that auburn tint comes from the birds that Great Uncle introduced eighty years ago. Do not read Dr Potts' account of the origin of the various types and colours. His book is too accurate and profound and one cannot afford to cast away what little romance may be left in the world. How lucky I am to be writing a specious sort of book where my own inaccuracy and shortcomings do so little to pierce the wonder and mystery of nature. I shall not describe the plumage of the Grey or the Red-leg – I am sorry if you pass one unaware as a result, but if you once see one you will always recognise it again and

The Ogridge

the Game Conservancy booklets fit so easily into the pocket if you want to sit outside the pen, as I think you should, and observe more closely.

NESTING

The partridge is a ground nesting bird and a prey to all that moves. Fox, rat, badger, stoat, weasel, magpie, crow, rook – all have their fill. The nest is, however, well concealed among low cover and the incubation period of about twenty four days sets a limit to the time of extreme danger. (A period of six or seven weeks may elapse between the laying of the first egg and hatching). You may think that that is an odd way to put it but when one is oneself looking for nests whether of game bird or pest one is always surprised at the number of empty nests one finds and at those where, once eye taken off for a day or two, only scattered egg shells remain for one's next visit. You must remember that I am unpaid, part time and an amateur! Personally there are only two periods when I have any very accurate idea of what is going on. The first is when the birds, having started pairing in February, become, as time goes on, very much attached to one small area or indeed one starts seeing only one trying to look nonchalant as one approaches. The other time, because all now becomes a sea of impenetrable grain, is when harvesting is under way and the first reports of young coveys start coming in. The Red-leg will sometimes make two nests and not only that but on occasion the cock will incubate the eggs in one, while the hen tends the other.

Having paired off from January onwards, depending on the weather, the birds secure their area of several acres and laying commences at the end of April. Wide variations occur in the number of eggs laid by the Grey and the Red-leg. You can look for as few as eight; as many as twenty. Eight to fifteen would be more likely. For the Greys, olive brown eggs; for the Red-legs, creamy buff with some reddish spotting. Our game farmer, who has an unequalled experience in handling partridge eggs – unequalled by any in the field that is – tells me that they come in every possible variation of colour, shade and size! Both Greys and Red-legs hatch about mid-June. Ascot day is accepted as the time of peak concern for the gamekeeper: torrential rain at that time may spell a poor season for the wild birds. Nevertheless, we had a very strong covey of Red-legs born at the beginning of a fortnight's steady rain and they are doing well. Probably the birds can put up with a great deal of wet and cold if insect food is abundant. Incidentally, one mentions Ascot day on the authority of the experts and I am sure that that is the red letter day.

It is surprising, however, the number of three to five week old birds just able to fly that the combine disturbs during harvest: I mean from mid-August until the second week in September. Ten young Red-legs were put up several times on 7 September; they were just able to fly and disappeared at once on landing in the stubble. Of course, these are second broods it may be said but there do seem to be a lot of them. In no way could we commence partridge shooting on 1 September were we to shoot wild birds. On that day there would be nearly as many immature birds as adults. No doubt predation, perhaps the weather, accounts for these late or second hatchings. We are glad to have them and glad that our lot is not finally determined on Ascot day!

THE CHUKAR AND THE OGRIDGE

The Chukar and the Red-leg/Chukar cross called an Ogridge, deserve a chapter to themselves because they loom so large in the world of the released partridge. When I talk of Red-legs throughout this book, I follow the convention and everyone understands me. What I am in fact talking about, I suppose, for most of the time, and it is as well not to confuse people by dwelling too long on it, is the Ogridge. There seems to be no work dealing with the Chukar or the Ogridge and I know that, as something of a fool among the partridge myself, I mention either at my peril. I use the name Chukar loosely. It could be a Chukar partridge, an Arabian Chukar partridge or the Game Conservancy say it may be one of the Rock partridges. It could be a sub-species of any of them. Whatever it is, crossed with the Red-leg, it produces a good laying bird and one which is well behaved in captivity.

The Ogridge has achieved a dominant position in the world of the released partridge. I do not know of any sporting difference between the Ogridge and the Red-leg. Both look much the same, fly in the same way and, I believe, taste the same. An expert could correct me perhaps? The game farmer estimates the difference between the Red-leg and an Ogridge at about two to one. That is to say, the pure bird costs double the price of the cross. However well one likes the Red-leg and the thought of a pure bird – I suppose one might call it 'the English Red-leg' now – the difference between three thousand pounds and six thousand for a thousand birds is too much to allow principles to be the guide.

Now it seems that a new influence on our sporting affairs may determine the fate of the Ogridge and the purity of the line. The EEC have it in mind to ban the release of the Ogridge into the wild. I believe this policy is designed to protect the native species from being swamped by foreigners: but did the Red-leg really swamp the Grey? I doubt it. Originally I assumed the opposite, that the EEC were so persuaded because the cross is not prolific. It seems commonly accepted that Ogridge rarely breed in the wild and when one is told this one does experience a revulsion at putting down a bird which has no role in nature's play but is merely to be a target for sportsmen. For that reason I welcomed the EEC's proposal and was heartened by the news that our birds were now 'almost pure'. Whilst I am never able to understand the Bible or the footnotes to my edition, it may be to this fickleness on the part of the Chukar that Jeremiah XVII ii refers: 'As the partridge sitteth on eggs and hatcheth them not'! It is difficult to imagine the cheerful Chukar or Sand grouse of the Middle East neglecting her duties in a manner to excite Jeremiah's notice. Indeed not, infers Mr Paddy Fetherston-Godley writing in the *Shooting Times* and *Country Magazine* on 14 September 1988. His timely article is an illustration of the little that is generally known of the partridge and in this particular case, the Ogridge. Much of what we think we know and which I repeat with an air of wisdom in this book, is supposition and rumour and very little, if any of it, has been committed to writing. Mr Fetherston-Godley is a man of considerable experience in rearing and showing partridge in England and Scotland and in observing them elsewhere in the world. He talks impressively of tagged birds and observation. He finds that the released Ogridge is no worse a breeder in the wild than the average released bird, and we all know that the average released bird does not do very well in a world that does not greatly favour partridge breeding. So if you rate released Red-legs as poor breeders, then the Ogridge is also a poor breeder. But Mr Fetherston-Godley can take us further than that with a persuasive accuracy of observation. He finds that the Ogridge is a rather better breeder than the Red-leg in the hills, which are akin to its proper habitat (on one side, I suppose), rather less successful on the chalky downlands of the southern counties.

So perhaps the Ogridge is here to stay. It is said by some that once in the wild, as it were, the cross will gradually die out. Whether this is said because it is thought that its inability to reproduce is such that it will inevitably decline or because it is thought that the stronger stock of wild Red-legs will predominate, I do not know. Mr Fetherston-Godley has gone a long way towards disposing of the first supposition and I can cast some doubt on the second because I know that there are very few Red-legs living naturally in our area, at any rate.

Are we due for a third species of partridge in our fields? Well, if Mr

The Red-leg, the Grey and the Ogridge

Fetherston-Godley is right, then this must depend upon the EEC in the first place, but in the second place it must depend upon the game farmers. These are stiff lipped men, the holders of many secrets. Those torn from Mr. Fetherston-Godley in the agony of the EEC's imminent policy are an example. Do others among them wink at each other when they hear the argument for and against the pure French bird and remark: 'I haven't seen a pure Red-leg for thirty years!' Are they rather like the farmer who had a bit of trouble with his tax return and with whom the tax man was desperately trying to make an appointment. Eventually in the course of a telephone conversation the tax man said: 'Well, I tell you what, I'll come and meet you at Wareham market next Thursday.' The farmer roared with laughter. 'Why!' he said, 'I haven't been to Wareham market for thirty years.' Too late he remembered that a weekly visit to that market had been among his tax free perquisites for the same length of time. But what about the pure Chukar cocks? Is their pedigree established since they were first brought to this country? One wonders if some are not a little mixed up by now. One does not know but I dare say there is a lot of experience and knowledge locked up in the minds of the breeders. Mr Fetherston-Godley's article shows that there is much to be said for the Ogridge and not much to be said for unfounded assumptions and deductions. Oh well! This book is full of them.

The birds themselves give some indication of their origin in their plumage. While the Red-leg has a speckled bib stretching from a darkish collar down across the crop area, the Chukar has a distinct black collar only. From these descriptions there will be slight variations according to the purity, if that is the right word, of the cross. We did have a batch which had grey legs and we suspected that they were immature. However, their legs remained that colour until they were released and indeed until some had been shot and by that time they must have been well over twelve weeks of age by any calculation. What we are seeking in our Red-legs is a good speckling from the throat down across the crop area. Again a cigarette taken outside one of the pens with your grimy copy of the Game Conservancy booklet on Red-legs may tell you just how much foreign blood there is in your birds.

THE STOCK

> the circling covey bask
> Their varied plumes, and watchful every way,
> Thro' the rough stubble turn the secret eye.
> *Autumn*, James Thompson

Should one have layers and breed one's own stock or have eggs or chicks or poults? I am sure I do not know. We may do a little rearing shortly because someone has expressed an interest in that side of it and has the land on which he can engage in that on his own account, as it were. If I had a keeper, I would turn him out into a field and tell him to get on with it, and I suppose he would know what to do. The Game Conservancy have produced a leaflet which sets out in a clear and concise manner how to govern the early part of a partridge's existence, but there is a lot of work and skill involved. I have never had anything to do with the raising of these birds and do not propose to talk of things of which I know nothing, at any rate where there can be no profit in my doing so. We are a syndicate of busy, working men – with one exception. I have the honour to be that exception and in constant work in the vermin line and in running the pheasant side of things, I find complete employment. Whatever the satisfaction of a job completely done, the labour and expense of a rearing programme can seldom be justified on a Shoot that is run by people in their spare time. Buying partridge poults is the easiest way of going about a Partridge Shoot and, although, as I have said, we may run a separate breeding venture, it will have to prove itself over a period of years before we come to depend on it.

Lively, well-nourished, bright of eye and unruffled of feather. Those are the things you should be looking for – in your supplier of course, not in the birds! If you get that in your birds as well, then you are in luck. If in addition you get plenty of feather round the head, and clean tail feathers, then you are still better off. However, you are mainly to be concerned with your supplier. If he is right, then the birds are likely to be good as well. You will scarcely see the birds on arrival because they are packed twenty or thirty to the crate and there will be eight or ten crates in the back of the Land Rover. Unless you were able to manufacture your pen gates of a size to fit these crates (usually 2 ft x 2 ft 6 in), the crates will have to be tipped side-ways to get them into the pen and it will be a dishevelled little covey that fly around the pen and scurry under the shelters. Your supplier will explain that they were kept in a wire enclosure while he hardened them off for the past two weeks, and that some have lost head feathers as a result, but no, he has not had a problem with feather pecking. Incidentally, breeders seem to manage this very well, or perhaps partridge are amenable little birds and we have never experienced any difficulty with feather pecking, even when the birds have been kept in the pens over four weeks – keeping the birds there too long does result in a filthy pen, particularly if there is much rain. However, it has to be said that our experience as far as Red-legs are concerned is with a cross. It is said that the pure Red-leg which the EEC would like to have as the standard product is more inclined to feather peck and is a more difficult bird to rear.

I have emphasized the nature of the supplier for a number of reasons. As I say, the first decent chance you get to look at the birds is when they are berserk on being released from their crates. Thus, you are in a difficult position to reject them if in fact they are found wanting. In any case, you probably have a number of other pens to fill. A good supplier will replace any that die without good cause and you will probably get a baker's dozen: well, one or two over the hundred. Then you must depend on your supplier to have hardened the birds off – this is particularly necessary whether the weather has been dry and hot, or wet and cold. I think it may be particularly difficult to harden birds off in hot weather; they probably need a sprinkler on them a few times in the last weeks. This, so rumour has it, causes them to preen and so to produce a waterproofing effect for the really wet days to come. Again, if it is wet and cold, the breeder must be tempted to keep his birds warm and dry all the time and if he does so a sudden exposure to downland weather will decimate them. A lot of people are breeding these days and no doubt some very good birds are reared. There are, I think, one or two things to beware of in the amateur breeder. Too many seek to reduce the cost of a Shoot by a side line that is not fully charted, and to which they are not fully committed. It must be very difficult to get the number of birds that you need, and at the same time, have enough to cover for emergencies. Thus it is very much easier in rearing for one's own Shoot to breed a greater number than is required and make a profit from selling the surplus, than to keep a market supplied. It is, in fact, only a surplus that is for sale. In the matter of weathering alone, how many see a large unused brooder house on the estate and believe that they have the perfect rearing and holding shed. So they may have, but unless they are dedicated suppliers of game, it is in the little matters like hardening off that they will fail.

You will rely on your supplier mixing wheat with the pellets in the fortnight before delivery. Our supplier brings a bag of pellets for each pen with him so that the birds may not be subject to any sudden change, and hitherto, we have mixed these then and there with wheat in the containers, but the birds do not have very long in the pens to get used to the wheat, so their early experience is important. Next year, we shall be feeding grain and pellets from separate containers to avoid the rapid emptying of drums by those seeking the pellets. No doubt those seeking amusement will continue to hammer the drums. Quite what the birds will make of the change, I do not know, but it is our hope that the tailings which we shall be feeding will prove very attractive to them. We are lavish with our pellets; food may be expensive, but it is not the major item in one's costs. To return to the supplier, I know it is hard to watch the man snatch a sandwich as two o'clock approaches: he has been on the road a good part of the morning, but it is a wondrous thing when the job is complete and you have three hundred birds penned and fed by three o'clock on a Sunday afternoon. One can take a shameful advantage of the supplier by asking him to tag the birds as they are caught up for delivery. Perhaps you will go to his place to help with this labour? We have not tagged to date and thought that there might not be much to gain from knowing which birds are wild or from last season since the latter have always been such a minority on our Shoot and, in any case, are largely those that go unscathed through or round the Guns. We have now had second thoughts and are inclined to tag next year. We shall probably tag in five different colours or numbers and that will account for the four points of the compass on the extremities of the Shoot and its centre. Shall we then from our records of the shoots form some idea of how much interchange there is between the pen areas and whether those on the far extremity are likely to come into the centre or disperse generally or simply disappear? Is the Northern pen empty because the birds have been harried off the Shoot, or have they slipped down, as we suspect, to the middle pens? If we do this then the additional information as to the wild birds will be a bonus. The cost will not be excessive. I understand that some of the plastic tags on sale can catch in the pen netting and thus add to the many, and unsporting, methods used by the partridge to escape his natural destiny. If tag you do then it is best done, as I am sure you will be aware, before the birds are released into the pens.

Nor is that all, because your supplier who is, no doubt, the breeder can go some way to answering all sorts of queries as a result of which you may be enabled to write an informed booklet on this subject, or at least appear as a knowledgeable man to your peers. He will tell you what is happening in the wide world outside; how many Shoots have lost their birds and how many are suffering from this or that, the year being what it is. If he is a keeper, he will tell you how his Shoot is doing; how many foxes he has accounted for this year, and what he does about rats. A quiet chat over a cigarette while the birds settle will be very rewarding.

I know that many people will say that you should go and see the birds before you order or, to be more realistic, before taking delivery. Probably you should, certainly if you can spare the time, but who has any of that these days? Again, when the partridge are ordered, you may well want three hundred on a certain day and two further deliveries of two hundred. It is no good just receiving a message from your supplier to the effect that he has encountered some unforeseen difficulty and cannot make delivery. He must be able to replace his losses from his own resources or through his contacts in the trade. Our own supplier lost a thousand birds this year through theft. A lot of them were destined for our Shoot: we had a worrying time. We were buying at £2.30 a bird, but at that stage we were quoted £5.00 by one breeder and £8.00 by another. We still had a few extra when delivery time came, and they were older and stronger birds than we had a right to expect. Our supplier had kept his side of the bargain!

We learnt a lesson this year as a result of the experience of two seasons. In order to build our stocks up before the season starts we have to crowd our pens: the number of pens available to us is limited by site availability and the requirements of the drive. There are not many suitable sites and for reasons connected with covey building a site can generally only accommodate one pen. Early in the season one wants to accommodate the bulk of one's birds in these pens and give them as long as possible in the pens. So we put thirty birds, say, to a pen and after a week release ten of them and put in another twenty releasing every few days after that. That will give you birds well attached to the site and released in good time to be fit, strong birds at the first shoot. We found to our surprise that in certain pens the first top up did very badly. Mostly we blamed that on the weather but after some study it became apparent that in this particular top up were some birds of a late hatching and noticeably younger than the earlier arrivals they had just joined. Birds being what they are the new arrivals were being bullied unmercifully. 'How good the new arrivals look', said a syndicate member who was struck by the compact circle of birds jugging, as it were, in a corner of the pen. Not at all! They were about to enter that state of dejection and decline that one recognises as the prelude to death and from which small birds never recover. If in doubt you call it death from pneumonia but there are other causes of death and starvation is one: and these birds were being starved. It was difficult to sort out; two pens were affected. In one we released most of the small birds because that was the convenient way it fell out and in the shelter of the release pen and outside these birds appeared to thrive. In the other pen we released the older birds and the younger birds set to on the food with a musical chattering. The older birds on being released felt litle call to remain near the pen and departed. The covey bond had not been formed!

So your supplier must be able to do one more thing: he must be able to say: 'There are your thousand birds!' and point to the first dozen pens or whatever he has. It means that he must put your birds to one side, delivering the first batch on the date agreed and keeping the first and second top ups until you are ready for them. You will not get birds from the same rearing pen in your pens, or I suppose it is rather a matter of chance whether you will or not, but all the birds will be of the same age and able to give as good as they get. Of course this is an added burden on the breeder which you may not realise he faces. If you empty your pen of birds between deliveries then it will not matter to you if the second delivery consists of younger birds. To empty the pen may be the better way to do things; the original callers belong to the original covey anyway and perhaps one should not try to keep that covey tied to the pen any longer. There is a strong temptation for one to do that. I suppose there is a lot about rearing that one does not appreciate. It had never occurred to me, before I heard a casual remark, that growth rates will vary with the amount of light and this decreases fast as winter approaches. Thus a ten week old bird in October is not by any means as good a bird as the bird that in September is ten weeks old. Well, I do not know, perhaps if you comment on the small progeny of October you will be told that they came from a very small strain of Chukar! We expect our birds to be not less than ten weeks of age on first delivery and we welcome every additional day.

RED-LEGS OR GREYS?

> How happy could I be with either,
> Were t'other dear charmer away!
> *The Beggar's Opera*, John Gay

Which birds you release depends on the land available and the type of cultivation. Red-legs thrive on cultivated stubble and the arable fields; Greys like some cover. Red-legs will shelter in woods and woodland belts while the Greys will spring from the rough grass of a new plantation. Otherwise, woodland generally forms a good boundary for a Shoot, through or beyond which, the birds do not pass. We are lucky enough to have a generous amount of stubble left for our use and mustard seed is scattered in wide swathes in the winter barley on wet days in July in order to provide a useful cover after harvest. We are, however, very short of root crops. We release about fifty Greys to about seven hundred Red-Legs. You might say that this is balanced in some ways by the natural coveys of Greys held on the Shoot, their extreme liveliness and the value placed upon one or two Greys in the bag.

Of course, I am asking for trouble in writing a chapter under this heading when I can barely distinguish a Grey from a Red-leg. What are the natural coveys of Greys? Well, there are wild coveys every year and some of these are on ground where partridge have not been seen for years. I have no doubt that these are descendants of Greys released on one or the other of our two partridge Shoots over past years. On our present ground, there were three or four good coveys at the beginning of the season, I will not be specific because one of the coveys at least was very much a boundary covey. With the help of fifty Greys released, we shot twenty, and we believe that there are still a fair number on the Shoot – or perhaps I should say near it! Will the wild birds drive away those released? That always used to be the problem. We think not: the original wild stock are still around on the Shoot and those released this year are there also, but they have quickly become shy and difficult to come to. In short, they seem to have merged satisfactorily. Whether there will be trouble at pairing time I do not know, but one has a strong feeling that when they meet around the hoppers in hard weather or in the swedes after next year's harvest, there will be no distinction between the wild and those released the year before. None that they can tell at any rate. The answer does not necessarily lie in a count of coveys next year because we know that stock will increase when conditions are right, whether it is wild stock or that which has been released. There has been a three year gap in releases on our present Shoot so there are no statistics available. Whether or not wild birds will refuse to accept those that have been released our experience, which as I say is of very limited numbers, is that nothing but good can come of a release in those small numbers at any rate, and a small number of Greys on open downland certainly go a long way! Our perimeters are wide open to accept any Greys that disdain our immediate hospitality and even on adjoining land they would be a bonus to us in filling that void. I know that the proposition that wild birds will drive away released ones was put forward in the days when wild birds were more numerous than any likely to be released and no doubt there was evidence for it. Now that releases are likely to exceed the numbers of the resident population, the converse is suggested; namely that those released will drive their wild brethren away. From what I have already said, it is clear that, although our experience is limited, we have no reason to fear that.

While I may not have spoken with any certainty about Greys, there is less still that I can say as to Red-legs. The difficulty here lies in the fact that the crosses we have been receiving have not been breeding to any extent. This year we shall have a nearly pure strain. It should be quite pure next year and perhaps we shall be counting the natural coveys of Red-legs. When that day comes, we shall learn if there is any question of those interfering with released birds or vice versa. The outcome does not worry us at all. In the meantime, though, should one be releasing Red-legs or Greys?

Not for anything would we do without our few Greys. They go off with a whirr and a clatter and by the end of the season they will fly a long distance. From the roots, if they are so kind as to be present, they whirr away in a curve and often with a swift vertical flight which gives several in the line a really testing shot. Anyone who achieves his left and right in such circumstances goes home in deep satisfaction. In fact, we shot about twenty last season but I suppose we had about a hundred on the ground to start with.

Red-legs are our bread and butter, keeping reasonably near the release pens, flying in small numbers and returning home in due course. If you put down four hundred Red-legs, then you can tell your Guns to expect their three sixty bird days. A foolish thing for me to say because I should be emphasising how much it is all going to depend on your ground and whether the farmer has a Gun in the Shoot and is prepared to suit you in the matter of the cultivations. It depends whether the badgers destroyed two of your pens, on the depredation of rats, of foxes, of human beings or weather. Nevertheless, if you are such a fool as to make promises to your syndicate, then you are better off doing it with a release of Red-legs than with Greys.

THE PENS

Wi' jay o' heart mid shooters start
   The whirren pa'tridges in vlocks;
while shots do vlee drough bush an' tree,
   An' dogs do stan' so still as stocks.
   An' let em ramble round the farms
   Wi' guns 'ithin their bended eärms,
   Rejäicèn vor the Harvest Hwome.
The happy zight, – the merry night,
The men's delight, – the Harvest Hwome.
   A Zong ov Harvest Hwome, William Barnes

We find a double pen very suitable for keeping partridge in – and as a method of release. It is good because when one lot of birds has gone, the incoming birds may be given the second half of the pen and further because when once released, birds use the second half for jugging. They are reasonably safe there for the first few days from foxes, badgers, dogs and corvids and, of course, the proximity of birds in the other section of the pen makes it an attractive place. Above all, however, the double pen is designed for release purposes, a matter with which I deal later.

   A team of three can erect a release pen on a Saturday morning if they have reasonable access to the site and that means following the combine. Otherwise, carrying pen sections, stakes, corrugated iron and tools along the bramble infested edges of cornfields can be a most exhausting task, though I may say, it has been done. It is even worse when one is asked to take a newly erected pen down and move it because on second thoughts a different site is preferred. Although pens are intrinsically mobile, they do prefer as they grow older a static existence. Often the ground is such that gaps between sections have to be reinforced by stapled chicken wire and gaps beneath by a good deal of hard earned soil. Access to the site is all important. If you can do the work in the spring, then the labour may be halved. What in spring is a soft maleable base becomes, for us at any rate, a rock hard area of chalk and flint in the summer. An added advantage of spring work is that the ground has time to firm up and grass has a chance to grow before the pen is used.

While the basis of the four sided pen has not changed in the history of our two partridge Shoots, the perfect construction is still a matter of evolution. Basically, each side of the pen is a ten by five or a five by five foot section comprising three six inch wide boards along the bottom with uprights and cross members of two by one timber. One end which, as I will show, becomes the centre of the double pen, has let into it a pophole. We have tried hardwood and we have tried marine ply but experience has proved that a solid metal plate, if you can get it, forms the best cut off for a pophole. It virtually never jams, is heavy enough to fall when the string is released and endures forever. From the pophole the release string runs to a staple on the top side timber and thence outside the roof netting to a point at either extremity of the double pen where it may be tied to a nail since you may have to leave the pophole open for some time. The string should not be left inside the pen otherwise a bird will sooner or later hang itself. Incidentally, the next time we build pens and this depends very much on such works of demolition within the neighbourhood as there may be, I hope that we shall build one or two ten foot by five foot by four foot high pens as opposed to the five foot high ones. This will make for some difficulty in entry, but entry is not so important with the automatic release system. The reason for the lower height is to reduce the height of the silhouette. A ten by five foot pen tends to stand out against the winter hedges on these hills. One accepts that a double ten by five by five foot pen is as much as most sites will stand. Here and there you may have more room to play with and a wider pen will be a great convenience. The bottom will remain green and firm despite the activity of the birds and the effect of heavy rain. You will find that there is room to get round the food shelter to catch the birds should that be necessary without crippling yourself and it will be easier to count them. We have a double pen of which the sections are ten foot by ten foot which is a pleasure to use. Even a few eight foot end sections (if you are making them) will give valuable extra space where a site allows.

The other piece of complicated machinery is the pen front: this is illustrated on p. 32. This is your door section and if you have a clear ten feet to play about with you can place the door squarely in the middle. This will allow you something over three feet on each side of the door so that a shelter can be fitted at either end of the pen without inconvenience. The door needs to be just over two feet in width and that not only allows you easy access with a bale of straw in an emergency, but will allow a crate of poults to be carried in without having to occasion them the loss of their self respect. Now the door is set above the base

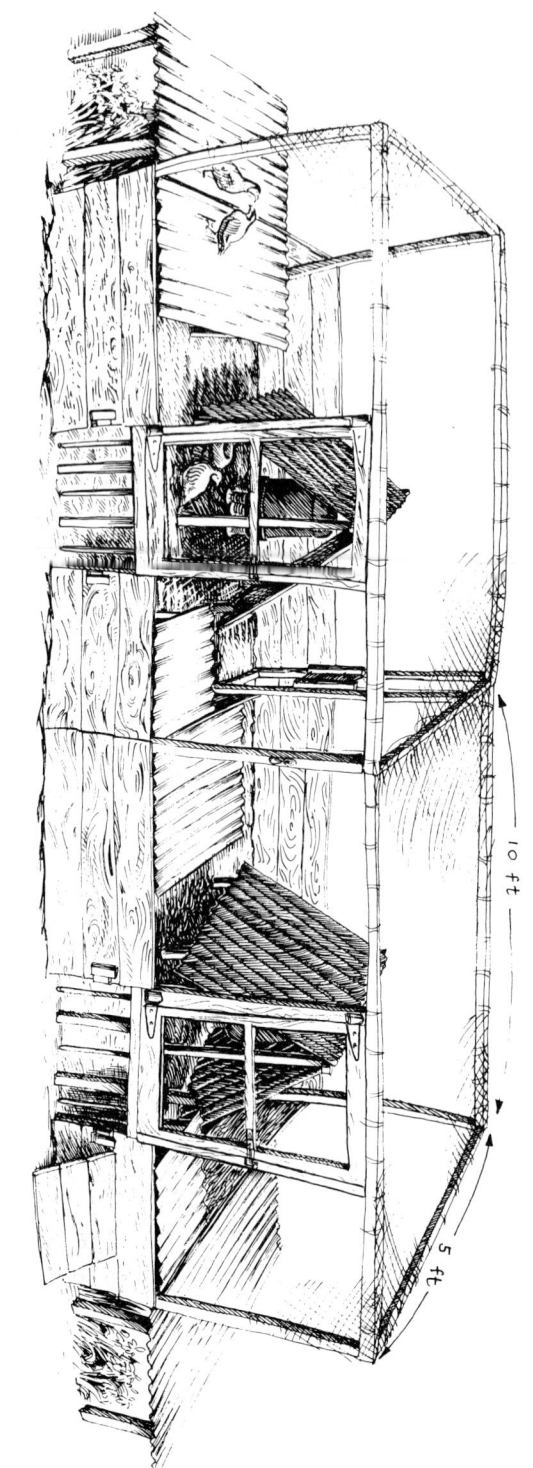

The Pen

boards and these are cut away as you can see from the illustration to provide a wide and commodious exit and entrance for the birds. This opening is fitted with anti-fox grids against which a sheet of marine ply may be held by a couple of pegs when the birds are to be kept in. The fox grid is the standard metal grid of the pheasant pen with rods $3\frac{1}{2}$in apart, but if you are making them up you can reduce the interval to $3\frac{1}{4}$in or less. Adult partridge in captivity pass easily through a three inch gap (we, in fact, set our metal rods in a wooden frame made from two by two). The grids we use are about ten inches high: they need not be so high but one does want to make the entrance as inviting as possible so that the birds will use the release section long after they are freed. Because we started the double pen system as an experiment, we have these release grids in various places on the different pens. It would be common sense to have them facing onto cover or against a hedge, but we are short of cover. It would probably be most convenient to have them in front because the last thing one does on walking away after a release is to uncover the grid on the release section (as a matter of fact I go away on tiptoe forgetting all about the covered grid!). Nor do the grids interfere with the inner or outer shelters when placed in front. We have found the birds very willing to use the grids while they have not appeared so keen, for instance, to use an intercommunicating pophole that has been placed under a shelter.

Each pen section should be covered in wire chicken netting of one inch mesh or less. If larger mesh has to be used then for one foot above the base boards along the promenade formed by the shelters some further protection should be provided: either a double mesh or a length of one or half inch chicken wire. It is at these points that the birds will stand to communicate with those outside: for whose use a bale of straw has been left or a shelter built. Often their visitors will be a covey of wild birds and the birds like to communicate cheek by jowl with each other and these facilities afford them the opportunity so to do. Coming up to such a pen this year I saw through my glasses what appeared to be a bird on the shelter with its head stuck in the wire. On closer examination, this turned out to be not one bird but two: each was strained towards the wire and minus its head. One also had a leg missing. A third bird was under the shelter inside the pen, also headless, having, in my view, come down from the shelter after it had lost its head. I remember a writer who warned of foxes which go round pheasant release pens doing something which provokes pheasants into sticking their heads through the wire. Those heads, so the writer said, were then removed by the fox. I had no doubt, therefore, that a fox sitting on the outer shelter had

Red-legs like to perch

caused these birds to put their heads through the wire since the mesh was large enough for them to do so: as they did no doubt out of curiosity in much the same way that a duck will follow the decoy dog. I take pleasure in my diagnosis, no doubt old hat to many people, because I am very fond of foxes and have found on stalking them that they very nearly do to me what was done to those birds. I have heard of other instances of heads being bitten off and the general opinion there, as it is of knowledgeable persons on our own Shoot, is that this is the work of rats! The same pen which is well away towards our boundary was plagued by badgers but had no rat problems as far as I know. Birds were still healthy and active there at the end of January, to no small extent perhaps because being rather far from the magic centre of our Shoot, they tended to go in the wrong direction on shooting days. At any rate, a one inch mesh wire was placed outside the existing one and there were no more incidents.

We like to staple the wire netting of the pens to the outside of the framework as partridge will do themselves an injury if they can, and could possibly snag themselves against cut wire stapled to the inside. I was therefore interested the other day to be told by someone that they always stapled to the inside to avoid birds being caught between the mesh and the woodwork, that is to say, by slipping down between the baseboards and the wire. No doubt there is something to be said for that too.

I prefer the gate to open outwards, though there may be more than one view about that also. It is helpful if there is an inner fastening; in fact it is something that I have to put on our pens if it is not there already. When one enters a pen, birds are apt to fly with sufficient force to knock a loose door open and it is surprising how quickly birds, which will spend ages wandering about in front of an open pophole, will take advantage of an inadvertent offer. On the outside we use a sliding bolt to close the door and generally tie a couple of pieces of wire around the uprights as well. This is a confounded nuisance to me and a second bolt would be as good a protection against animals and vermin. However, my head keeper has learnt from experience that padlock and chain does not deter the two legged thief and only results in damage being caused to the pen. At the same time, he feels that a bolt makes it too easy for them. Thus the great inconvenience that frequently sees my finger snagged on a wire is all designed as a friendly welcome to the intruder and I do not expect, were I to show my head keeper a condemnation of his method in print, he would wish to alter it to preserve my finger.

When we set up our original Shoot, some of our pens were of weld mesh and without base boards. We ran fertiliser bags around the base giving a fairly high cover against the elements. In consequence, our shelters were high and commodious to give the birds the view from the top that they needed. Subsequently, we changed to baseboards which are a good deal neater and less conspicuous and as a corollary the corrugated shelters inside ran across the pens at a height of one foot or one foot six inches. Since we were then also using single pens it was simple to fix the iron shelter on two horizontal stakes which protruded on the outside of the pen to support another sheet of corrugated iron. All went well until this year when the advent of the double pen led to the shifting of shelters with the result that the shelter at one end of the double pen faced east and at the other end west. Unfortunately, at that stage in our development it was in the pens whose shelters faced west that a number of poults were placed when driving rain, coupled with tenderness on the part of some of the birds, caused losses. The damage was heaviest in the least exposed pens of the valley. At first we were of the naive opinion that this was because the wind was so strong higher up the hill the shelters were more effective: and certainly those pens had better drainage. A sheltered position is a matter of fact and experience, rather than of estimation or calculation, it seemed. Later we noticed that some of the worst affected pens had only two baseboards to a height of one foot instead of one foot and six inches. Bales of straw placed in front of the less hospitable shelters proved their worth, but the low shelters combined with the filthy ground made it very difficult to check the condition of the birds.

In the future we hope to ensure that all pens have three baseboards and that calls for a shelter of the same height. A bale of straw in front of an eighteen inch shelter makes for a comfy abode. It would be as simple a matter to put the corrugated iron shelter itself on two bales of straw: the further advantage of this greater height is that it will allow a feeder to be introduced beneath the shelter. That will depend on the type of feeder in use but a standard slit feeder can easily be cut down to fit on bricks under such a shelter. In fact, we have avoided any such necessity by the use of individual shelters for all our feeders. My head keeper does not like straw: whether because of the awful things he has read about Aspergillosis or because of his experience of that disease I do not know but straw bales are out! They have the added drawback for us of providing homes for vermin and of being almost impossible to lift when thoroughly soaked. We have considered shelters with a flap coming down the front and one of our shelters is so made up at the moment, but I do not think it has a great deal to recommend it. I may be prejudiced because my efforts at fitting corrugated iron into the available space were not altogether successful, certainly not something that the Prince of Wales would rave about. Incidentally, an angle grinder is a wonderful tool for cutting corrugated iron and most farms seem to have one. The other idea was to run one of the new type large fertiliser bags from the back of the corrugated iron. To prevail against wind and rain this would have to be stiffened at the bottom by a fencing stake and that to some extent would detract from the curtain effect desired.

It would be very nice to abandon corrugated iron which is difficult to cut, sharp-edged and noisy. I am told that partridge dislike the sort of noise produced by corrugated iron when they walk upon it and that it is best insulated by a layer of earth – just another complication! Perhaps the best material would be marine ply, although it is expensive. At any rate, a wooden shelter covered by roofing felt might be a great improvement. It should be about 2 ft 6 in wide by 3 ft in length and, as I have emphasised, 18 in in height. It would be good if it could be canted slightly to allow rain to drain over the side of the pen. Half of each exposed front should be boarded to provide winter protection for the small huddle of birds that twenty or more partridge present. The other two sides would be protected by the base boards. Beneath would be ample room for the cut down feeder and a tray of pellets when appropriate. It would be splendid to have such shelters free standing or lightly pegged down in some temporary manner. It is nice to be as specific about such designs as I have been: a luxury which I can seldom afford in executing my own engineering schemes, the design being heavily influenced by events during the course of the work. A member of our syndicate is a carpenter by trade and that makes all the difference.

I am not yet going to advise a coop, although you may think I am getting precious near it. The idea of a solid floor appeals very much to us at the end of a wet season but we are too worried about vermin to try it, so perhaps someone else will? I rather suspect that partridge would disdain such conventionality and jug outside.

Not only will the double pen need shelters adjacent to each other inside and out, but in the centre communication will be required between the two parts of the pen so that those released or awaiting release or merely jugging in the release section may converse with those remaining penned. For this purpose we further complicate things as far as any explanation of our system is concerned by placing a shelter at the other end of each pen or, if you like, one on each side of the middle section. In fact, since these are for communication only, and so as not to obscure the pophole between the two sections of pen, we use small 2 ft by 2 ft sections of corrugated iron which we call 'stools'. Thus, a double pen has an outer shelter, against it at each end an inner shelter and a stool against each side of the middle portion.

The roof of the pen should be of good quality mesh. We use a nylon net which we thought was quite good but even good netting ages, and a dog got through two of ours. Apart from normal defence purposes, the net may have to bear a heavy burden of snow during the winter. These nets can be effectively and neatly tied down using the plastic tags that horticultural merchants sell for use with garden nets. Baling twine is a good deal easier to cut and replace if a net has to be removed but I think most efficient of all is a line of short galvanised nails driven into the top rail of the pen. The net can easily be stretched over these nails and for double security, a length of twine may be run along, twice round each nail, above the net.

There is nothing new on earth and one is always completing the full circle. I am going to end this chapter by quoting the method of release for Hungarian partridges advocated by the manager of what were at that time the I.C. Game Estates, the reproduction of whose advice I had the

Netting tied down (here by plastic tags)

Netting stretched to nails and a length of twine run along

advantage of reading in Captain J. B. Drought's book *Partridge Shooting* which itself was published in 1936.

> For each seven or eight brace of birds prepare a pen sited on the sunny side of a good hedge, or in a dell hole, or in a strip of narrow covert bordered by arable land, or in a clearing just inside a covert. The pen should be 24 ft square, staked at every 6 ft with 7 ft 6 in stakes driven 18 in into the ground. It should be close boarded at the bottom (galvanised sheeting can be used instead of boarding) to the height of 2 ft from the ground with the boarding sunk 6 in into the soil; and above this boarding the enclosure should consist of 4 ft netting of 1 in mesh, stapled to the posts. The top 12 in of the netting should not, however, be stapled, as the loose flap thus left will prevent cats climbing into the pen. A strand of barbed wire should be laid flush with the ground all round the pen, to prevent foxes digging under, and another barbed wire strand where the boarding joins the netting, as an additional protection. Both these strands should be stapled to the posts. A half door must be provided, above the boarding, for the use of the keeper. In a pen of this description partridges can be kept with confidence for three weeks or longer before release.

SITING THE PENS

> I sometimes think I'd rather crow
> And be a rooster than to roost
> And be a crow. But I dunno.
> Anon.

There is not much advice to be given in the abstract about siting the pens, even were I qualified to give it. If you are a member of the Game Conservancy then they will arrange for a representative to come along and advise generally about your proposals and their advice as to sites will be well worth having. The trouble is that each Shoot has its own requirements. Not only will the lie of the land be different but the character of the farming and the extent to which the Shoot may obtrude on the farming interests must vary. However, I know what we do and what we would like to do and my recital of this may not be entirely irrelevant.

The ideal Shoot for hill shooting lies along one or more deep narrow valleys: not at all the sort of thing you find around the corner. We did have one on our last Shoot: this was situated on a farm of about two hundred acres which was on the perimeter of nearly a thousand acres of rolling downland. The owner of those acres saw a partridge shoot as a valuable extension of the sporting rights which he held not far away; adding, as is always the case with partridge, length and variety to his shooting season; perhaps work for the dogs too, on walking up days. The two hundred acres were joined in to round things off.

My head keeper got some pens erected on the top land but spent a long time pondering over the drives and their connecting links – you must drive partridge somewhere where they will not get lost: the aim is not to drive them off your property. In the end, we started moving the pens to positions overlooking the valley on the smaller property and to within range of a high hedge wich led from the valley. Soon, practically the whole Shoot was housed and centred on the two hundred acres which had been joined in. There just were not the hedges or the contours to provide the centre and the shooting positions on the larger area. On this small site the Guns commuted easily, a little too easily perhaps, up and down the valley. The shooting was very good, or rather, the sport was. For reasons unconnected with the site or the quality of the Shoot we had to close this down after two seasons.

That was an ideal Shoot providing good high birds and for easy placing of the Guns. Above the valley and set back on each side were the pens, their position, as ever, being decided by the suitability of the ground and the nature of the cultivations rather than by free choice. On one side two pens were set six hundred yards or so apart against the fence running along the top of the valley at its junctions with cross hedges. Two hundred yards back along one of these cross hedges would be a supporting pen making a rough triangle of pens. On the other side, five pens were situated behind the hedge lining the valley, backed by two placed half way up a hedge at right angles to the first at one end, a further pen centrally situated way back in some rough ground and at the other end one was placed so as to feed the rough hedge leading from the valley. One could have improved this by making use of depressions in the ground where there was rough cover or by using the bases of pylons further back, but as the land was cultivated the pens had to be in positions where our regular visits would not cause excessive damage. Those useful little pits which occur here and there in the downs are very attractive sites as are pylon bases, but the need to site the pens so that the birds can see around them does make a pen in such a position an obvious cause for remark and the downs are a very public place! As it was, it was possible to put twenty or thirty birds up at a pen and watch them fly across the valley to the other side. Fifteen minutes later they would be back.

In that case, the community of birds lived largely on each side of the valley. I doubt if they had territory and there is no doubt that until shooting commenced they tended to pack. Nevertheless, it was obvious to the birds that those few acres were home and that friendly country lay within the circle of their pens. Nor were they driven out at each shoot.

Our present position on a much older Shoot is not perhaps so satisfactory. Here, instead of a periphery of birds being driven into the centre, we have one half of a valley at one end, really more of an escarpment with hills opposite and close to it, a generous hill along one side and corn fields with the bonus of roots or mixed kale and roots on the other side. This time our main calling power comes from the main pens along a hedge that goes across the centre of the Shoot. At the valley's edge we have a further pen, two more on the generous hillside, and one about five hundred yards back from the centre hedge. We can push birds back from the centre hedge and bring them back over it: but that is not exciting shooting. From the roots there are wandering Red-legs and volatile Greys (there is a mobile pen for Greys there) and that gives us a good drive as the birds come back to the centre. From the hillside the birds come well and fast down to the centre pens again. Into the valley or over the escarpment we get high fast birds which tend to fly the contours and which go largely unscathed. Further along the valley, but still within hearing of their neighbours, we have two further pens, their siting conditioned by available cover and while these present some high birds, they lack true anchorage at the moment and are inconsistent. Next year, two further pens will be erected making a closer link for these outposts and we hope that more of a community spirit will emerge.

So you see, our Shoot is by no means ideal but sufficient calling power not only from penned callers but from coveys released and domiciled, as we hope, to the rear keep our act together. However, it is a near thing. One would like to say that every pen should be sited on, or near, a good but very private farm track. That is not likely to be possible and in our own case communication is very difficult. Beating distances around the periphery are long and effective transport of the beaters difficult to arrange and while, as I say, these things are to be taken into account when planning the Shoot it must seldom be possible to arrange the siting of the pens to meet the problem. It may, however, be that having found the perfect site for each pen, the difficulty of blanking in and beating from that site renders it useless.

Having found an appropriate piece of rough ground, one often has little choice as to how or where to site the pen within it. My own head keeper is a man of naval tradition and has a team of willing helpers. His pens are apt to be hewn from the rock if that is the only way that a shipshape result can be obtained. Maybe he is right but, employed as I am as a sort of sanitary man, I do find that pens which have escaped the level and lie at an angle are the best drained and longest wearing. Even when loose earth has been piled at one end to make a level base above the surrounding land, I find that the patter of tiny feet on a base of guano and pellets quickly makes an impermeable surface where water and filth gather.

Of course, you will want your pen facing south. Our experience is that the most sheltered southerly aspects have proved the wettest. It is true that those of our pens lying in such a position are in a slight curved east to west declivity or valley, but, although there is rising ground at each end, the downland rain drives horizontally through all. I noticed recently that some of the worse affected pens had only two lines of base board instead of the regulation three, so that probably had something to do with it also. On the fully exposed hill-sides, where pens have been placed on the north side of a bare hedge running roughly east to west, the effect seems not too bad. Perhaps the strong winds also dry the ground out quickly! At any rate, the birds are not in the pens long enough to benefit much from the sun, although they can quickly die at that stage from cold rain. It may be said that those using the pens to jug and feed in after release would prefer a sunny aspect. A pen situated on the north side of a downland hedge is a very different kettle of fish to a pen sited on the north side of a deep wood or high ground. One must beware of the gift of a site where the corn does not grow very well because of a lack of light. Birds placed there will wander off to warmer climes.

I do not know what keeps partridge at home and I suppose this book is an account of the efforts made at one Shoot to provide all the facilities and the environment that birds could wish for. One hears a great deal and no doubt there is a lot one does not hear and does not observe but I am impressed with two admonitions with regard to achieving a satisfactory result. The first is that partridge should not be over shot. They will of course be harried on a shooting day because it is often necessary, depending on the nature of the Shoot and the distance which the birds have to fly on the various drives, to return birds which have already been driven in one direction – but there should be rest between shooting days. If the main shoot takes place on three days, then that cannot be excessive. If there are more than three shoot days, then one should be looking to leave certain pens untouched on each occasion. In other words, one needs to have available a day and a half's shooting on the estate for each shooting day so that only two thirds of it is disturbed on any one shooting day. The second point which is perhaps more germane to this chapter is the need, in my view, to preserve the immediate area of a pen as a sort of sanctuary. Obviously one has to beat through and past such an area but I do not think the birds should ever be shot within a few hundred yards of the pens. On our own Shoot, this object is not achieved. In a year or so I think it may be as other drives become available, although whether the experts would agree with me entirely on either of these points I do not know.

Partridge manors on these downs are open, blowy places within distant view from public footpaths and roads. It is wise to place pens where children are not likely to explore or the ignorant destroy. A good site under a pylon may prove too open to view while a site under the north

A discreet siting on the north side of a hedge. Virginia Murray

side of a hedge may be inconspicuous. By using a dark creosote a pen can be made to merge with a background of blackthorn while care with feeders will stop them standing out like sore thumbs. Our metal drum feeders are painted a dull green and their tops, originally multi-coloured, are in the process of being painted grey. A very dark grey or black might be better for both. Green can be an obvious colour once the leaves have fallen: certanly not lost to view in blackthorn country. The plastic water containers and rat baiters are a problem as plastic does not take too readily to paint: the rat baiters are best left untreated, they will be hard enough to find after a month's hedgerow growth. This year we are going to try several ways of painting the plastic drums in an effort to get the paint to stay on. The water containers, since they are static, could be placed in black dustbin liners or green garden sacks – we shall see! Those who are able to obtain black plastic drums have the laugh on us! Each year we use creosote, as a general preservative, to deter foxes and as a general measure of hygiene. The creosote is best put on in good time as it scorches the grass and partridge are susceptible to creosote poisoning.

An important point I have not touched on is that of the view from the pen. Partridge are only penned so that they may acquaint themselves with a territory which is to become their own. They need a pen

Siting the Pens   45

with a view and, as mentioned in the chapter on pen construction, a stand which may be a straw bale, from which to view. A partridge should be able to stand on his bale or upon the shelter within the pen and look all around him. Of course, a hedge on one side may close much of his view – but not all of it. We like to think of the birds examining the country around them, listening to the calls of their neighbours and perhaps, at the bottom of the hill or across the valley, identifying an industrious community of their fellows and having at the back of their minds the knowledge that they can always visit there.

I know that it is said that release pens should be moved a few yards between batches of birds and I am quite sure that that is a splendid thing to do. Our pens are not designed for this and the sort of land we have is not conducive to regular moves. I have said earlier that a team will take half a day, perhaps, to put up a pen and that must seem like slow progress to those who are in the habit of moving their pens at intervals. Our pen building is however invariably a task of levelling and building up, and regular moves are therefore not possible. To some extent, our double pen alleviates the need to move. Putting down two or three hundred birds in twelve or more pens, cleaning the water containers and topping up the feeders is a long job. To move pens, were they built for that purpose, would call for considerable labour. However, this policy must be balanced against the risk of disease and our admitted susceptibility to mud and filth. A lighter pen with a simpler type of shelter would make such a move more practical. It is also said that pens must be removed before shooting: I do not know why. Perhaps if the Guns are going to shoot at the site of the pens this would be an advantage. If pens have to be moved to clear the land for cultivation, then I wonder if partridge should be released at all, obviously there is no plan for them in the scheme of things. Our pens, other than those which follow the roots, stay put and we hope will provide cover for any birds wishing to take advantage of them. Certainly in mid-January there were still birds feeding in one of the pens and using the release sections. At the end of March one of a pair crouched in a release section as her mate flew off, startled by my approach.

Finally, two small matters. If you happen to site your pen on a badger run, my experience is that the badger will continue to use the run as though no pen was there. Perhaps that is a slight exaggeration – but my meaning is plain. If you are going to saturate the ground with high protein pellets and good wheat, do not be surprised if the badgers empty your feeders, untie the knots when the feeders are tied to posts and eventually, enter the pen in a very untidy fashion and eat your callers. If

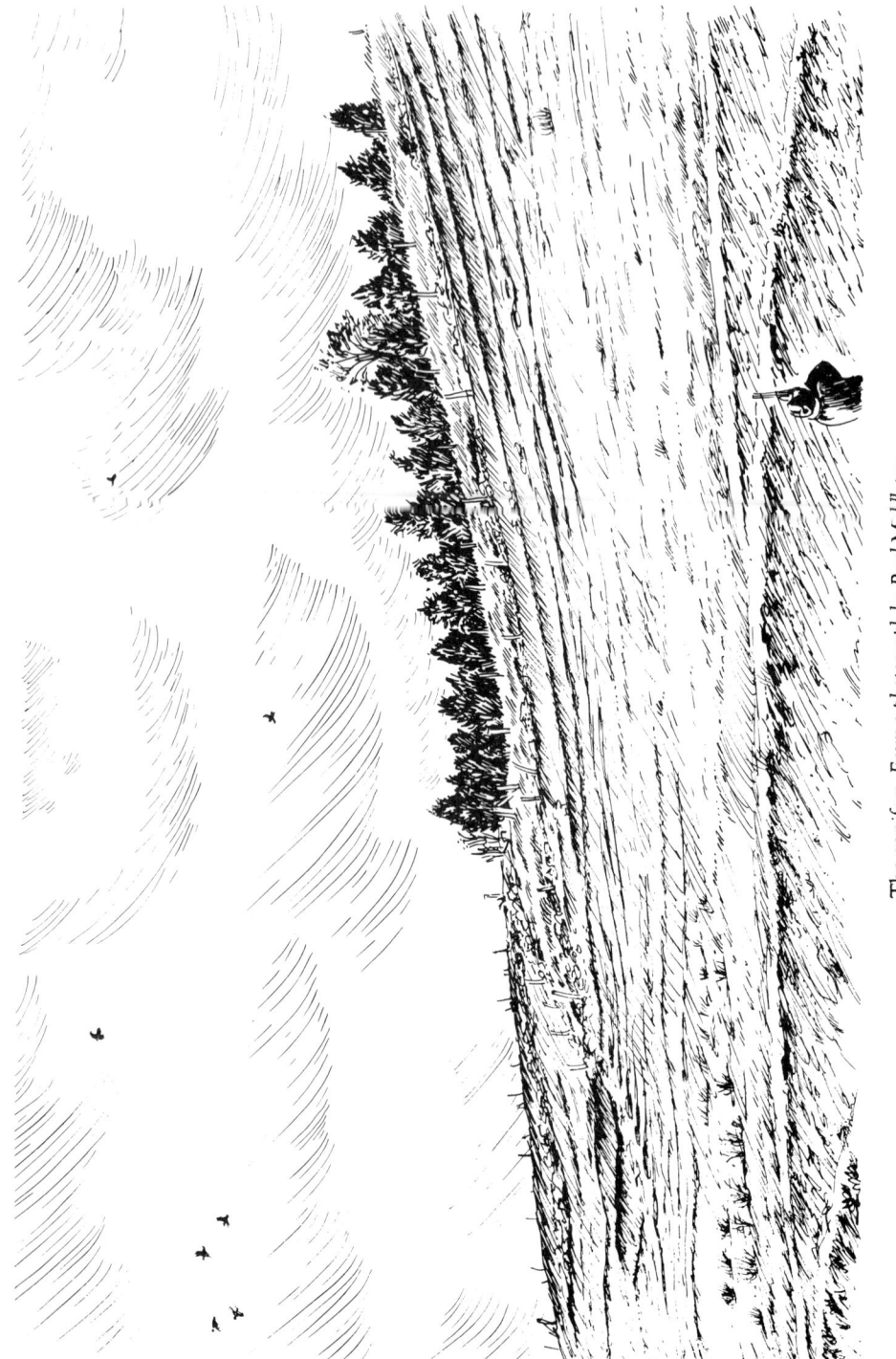

The conifers. From a photograph by Paul Middleton

you must site the pen near badgers (we have to) an electric fence will give you some protection. I am not sure about the badger, he is very inclined to accept an electric shock as a hazard of everyday life – or so I have been told by those who find the electric netting round their strawberries neatly tied in a bundle when they get up in the morning! Our experience has not been so bad. Last year we had a bad attack and we had to abandon that particular pen. Unfortunately, the attacker, or attackers, moved on and while they entered no other pens, they did a great deal of general damage emptying and upsetting feeders. This year three rows of electrified wire round the pen most at risk seem to have been effective. I see that the badgers have been busy enough in its vicinity. Next year we thought we would have several electric netting fences in the hope that this would see an end to the problem. I discussed with the shepherd the practicality of cutting the electric netting to the required lengths and he was helpful as always: 'You'll need a repair kit,' he said, handing me a plastic bag, 'Because the badgers are sure to make holes in it. Whatever you do, don't put it down across a badger run 'cause Brock will go straight through it.' Certainly our experience has been that once they get started, badgers are difficult creatures to deter.

Secondly, the pen should not be so close to a hedge or wall that one cannot get around it. One must be able to get round it for ratting purposes, while sometimes on a single pen where the pophole is on the side where the hedge or bank is the alley, so formed, can be roughly wired over to assist in the release.

FEEDING

> Some hae meat an canna eat
> And some wad eat that want it
> But we hae meat and we can eat
> An sae the Lard be thankit.
> The Selkirk Grace as attributed to Burns

We like to have four feeders to a pen: one inside each part of the double pen and one at each end outside. It should be possible for several birds to feed at each feeder. In addition, feeders are placed at other quiet places attractive to the birds and where it is convenient to us for them to congregate. Our feeding system is at a transitional stage: like most people running a partridge shoot, we were satisfied that our system was the best for us – until we visited Mr Keith Langdown's Shoot in Dorset and had a talk with him.

THE STANDARD SLIT FEEDER

Recently, we have fed from standard five gallon tin drums cleaned and painted inside and out. The top is cut off and replaced by the slightly wider top of a plastic drum. This fits securely and it is easy to refill the drums. The partridge extract the grain from the drums by pecking at four vertical slits cut at the base about one inch from the bottom and extending upwards for about four inches. The width of the slits is about $3/16$ in and they can be conveniently cut with an angle grinder. The object, which is always the subject of experiment, is to keep the grain inside the drum but easily available in small quantities to the birds pecking at it. When badgers are troublesome, a wire from each side of the lid can be run through holes bored at the bottom, but not into, the drum. That keeps the lid secure although it does not necessarily ensure that the drum remains on the estate! The drums are mounted on four bricks; if you can get hold of bricks from an electric storage heater you will find that they fit very nicely under the rim of the drum leaving

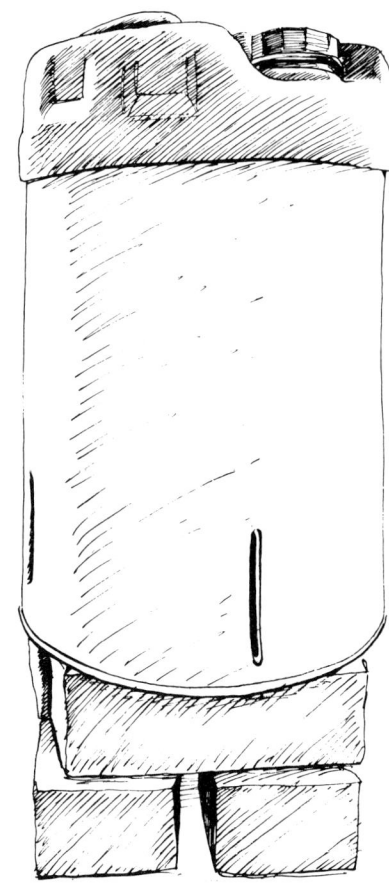

The standard slit feeder

nothing sticking out for rats to climb onto. As I say, there is such a drum in each section of the pen and when the poults first go in, a tray of pellets is placed under one of their shelters. I suppose that that is the exception to the rule that birds feed only from a standard feeder throughout the Shoot.

It was our aim last year to cut down drums which would then fit under the shelters in the release pens, giving food in dry places and carrying over to become good winter feeding spots. In the early stages of release, the drums always contained pellets mixed with good quality one year old wheat and as this was taken it was replaced by wheat alone. There was a major snag here as the birds learnt to peck out the wheat grains to get at the pellets. Certainly they learnt how to feed on grain and they learnt how to extract it but the waste was excessive. That, as I go on to relate, was not a serious matter in the light of our feeding policy.

FAULTS. Apart from high winds blowing the tops off, the remedy to which I have already mentioned, and which means that rain enters and spoils the contents, the drums can be blown off their bricks by the wind, particularly when they are half empty, and the result is the same. The drums are susceptible to being knocked over and rolled by badgers: I think we have had a very quiet year as far as interference by badgers is concerned and only in one case was persistent damage done. There we reduced the outside feeders to one which we hung from a cross-bar and not only did we have no further trouble, but the birds held very well at that spot. It is not easy to hang open top drums as they tend to cave in when laden. It is best to put a thick wire across the diameter and hang from that. It is important, also, to take defensive measures as soon as the first hint of trouble is spotted: an electric wire, perhaps? Once a badger achieves success at one pen, he will visit them all. I think that the worst fault of the split sided drum is that rain penetrates the slits, particularly later in the season when they are not used so much and those left in position for winter feeding, or not removed when their work is completed, need to be thoroughly cleaned out and dried before storing or reuse. The use of shelters over these feeders should greatly assist in this respect.

THE WIRE BOTTOM FEEDER

A couple of years ago, we used wire bottomed drums fixed to short posts driven into the ground at an angle of about forty five degrees. This angle is chosen, as I understand it, because the partridge will not look up to feed as the pheasant does. There is a lot to be said for this method. Armed with a number of squares of half inch chicken wire or its modern equivalent you can pad the hole at the bottom of each drum until you achieve the optimum flow and each time you fill you can vary this as you wish. Our wire bottom feeders in use for pheasants are very satisfactory and remain perfectly dry and useable from one year to the next. Those set at an angle for partridge should be equally successful.

FAULTS. Our neat and orderly array of wire bottom feeders were not successful because someone told the badgers how to extract the wire bottoms from these drums by the use of force and they ruined a good number of feeders.

The Game Conservancy illustrate in their booklet, *Red-legged Partridges* (Booklet 18) such a drum slung at the appropriate angle against a

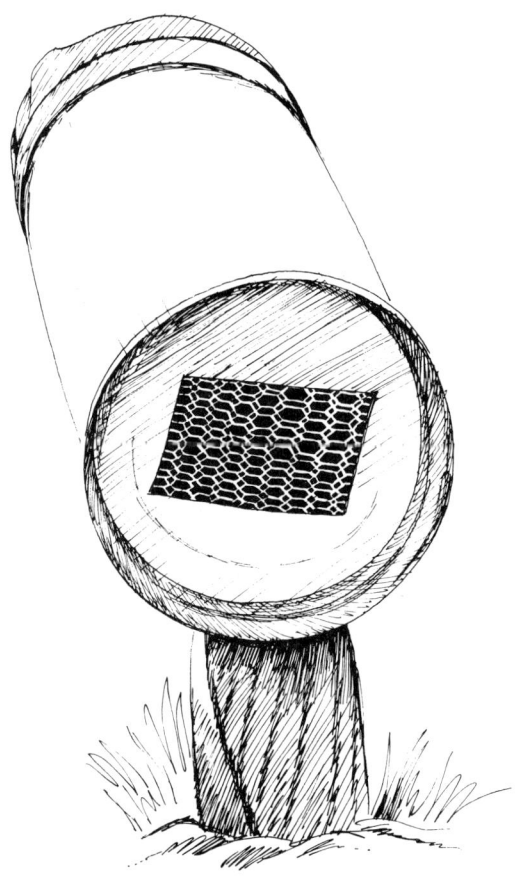

The wire bottom feeder

straw bale. In the right circumstances, that seems a good method of setting them up but we are rather against the use of straw bales mainly because we find the bales very difficult to move after a winter's rain and when the young corn sprouting in the spring makes transport difficult. They are also difficult to dispose of.

THE GAME CONSERVANCY LETTER-BOX FITMENT

The Game Conservancy sell a letter-box type of fitment which can be bolted on to a drum so that the birds can feed directly from the drum without its contents spilling out. I do not know how that works with partridge but it should work very well since it offers an unlimited supply of food readily available, which is just what we want, and that is coupled

52   Partridge for Sport

with safe and dry storage. It is, I think, rather expensive and therefore I have had no practical experience of using it. Anyone setting up a a Shoot and investing in new equipment might well consider fitting these for dispensing wheat or pellets. I should think it difficult to fit these particular fittings to anything other than an open top metal drum because after the hole has been cut for one it has to be bolted in, which requires access and having cut the top off a plastic drum we have not yet found a satisfactory cap for one.

THE HOSE-PIPE

By inserting a section of plastic land drain into the bottom of a plastic drum, the food can be run out onto a flat surface placed at such a distance from the end of the pipe as to allow the desired amount of food to be available. The surface may be a shallow pan or four or five bricks set to give a level surface. It is simple to fix the plastic drain into a plastic container using a drill and circular hole making saw and the feed remains dry and available. The drum must be supported either by being fixed to a post or suspended from a gallows. It may be placed on a shelter and the pipe run through that to a pen beneath. We used a couple with success for tailings: the rough nature of tailings demands an easy flow and the movement of a suspended drum helps to provide a good supply on the surface beneath.

FAULTS. Where there is too much movement there may be a danger of the feed going to waste. I imagine badgers would learn fairly quickly the right sort of swing for best results but I do not know if they would bother much about tailings: we experienced no difficulty in our limited experiment. The feed would be readily available to rats and small birds and unless fed through a shelter, the feeder would probably need protection from rain.

THE OWEN TICKLER

A devilish device, I feel, having made up fifty of them but one which makes cleanings or tailings available to the birds and offers greater security from waste and vermin than does the hose-pipe. The drum is designed for hanging and three four-inch sections of plastic agricultural drainage pipe are inserted in the base. Each piece of tube has a circular

The Owen Tickler

plate suspended from it onto which the feed falls. The plate is held about ¾ in. from the pipe. I found that twine provided the most efficient method of fixing the plate to the tube and our experimental ones were so made responding with an easy rock to any tap and ensuring a steady fall of tailings. However, I have now reached that honourable age when one takes off ones' glasses to thread a needle and I find plastic coated garden wire much easier to use. One can get through quite a lot if one has a box of cut tubes, plates and wire and sits in the armchair of an evening.

This method not only allows the small seed and split grain of the cleanings to be readily available but it allows the chaff and shorter lengths of straw to be blown, pecked or shaken away. Each of the covered galleries from which these drums depend has a staple at the end of its cross bar and the drum can be taken out and hung from this while it is being refilled. Yes, I am afraid we do feel that these feeders should be under shelter! The plates that we use are of metal. We started by using the cut ends of cat food tins which are very satisfactory, though I do not suppose they would last very long but we are now using a disk cut from more substantial metal. No doubt a plastic disk would do as well.

FAULTS. My wife sees me washing batches of drums, priming them, painting them, cutting lengths of plastic drainage pipe, fixing metal discs (already cut for me), painting the tubes and putting the whole lot together and she laughs a scornful laugh at the thought of the labour I am recommending others to undertake. Indeed, the labour is extortionate, but we hope that our feeder, once made, will last a few years. The system is designed for cleanings or tailings as they may be called, about which I shall write later. It would be sad if anyone dedicated the time necessary to building such feeders before securing his supply of cleanings.

THE McDONALD FAST FOOD FEEDER

This delightfully simple artefact (in comparative terms) consists of a plastic drum cut so that the top few inches forms a lid. This is forced onto the body of the drum which has slits cut into it at the top in order to accommodate this lid. Because the lid has a natural inclination to come off straight away, a pulley like arrangement with some baler twine through the centre of the lid to a loop of wire at the centre inside bottom of the drum ensures that the weight of the drum, when hung by the twine, is transferred to the lid so that it remains firmly fixed. By placing a four inch plastic collar around the inside top of the cut drum, this manœuvre with the baling twine can be avoided and the lid simply fitted over the collar and this, the Mark 2 version, is thus enabled to stand without help on bricks. The collar does not provide a good waterproof union as at present designed, but as we would only use it under our feed shelters this is immaterial to us. The feed is obtained by the birds through a letter-box cut in each side of the drum. I find it simplest to cut two two-inch diameter holes at three-inch centres and then to roughly even out the figure of eight hole thus produced. In case you feel like giving up at this stage, I should say that this work is no more than you would have to undertake if you were to fit a couple of the Game Conservancy's letter-box fitments to any open-topped plastic drum and

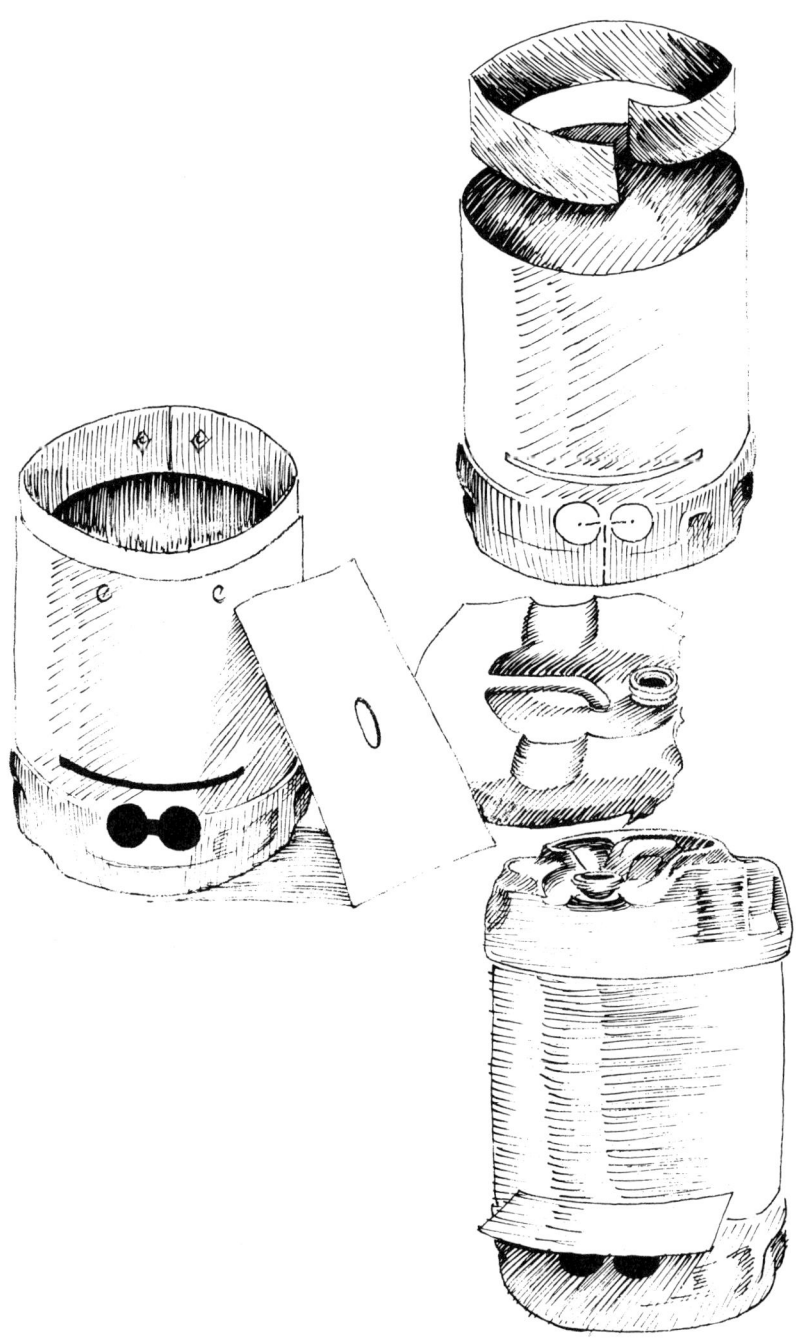

McDonald Fast Feeder

the drum ought to be open-topped whatever the system to make for easy filling. Now, the bottom lip of the roughly rectangular holes is two inches from the bottom of the drum. Half an inch above this opening, and extending on either side of it, a ten inch saw cut allows a flat piece of plastic to be pulled through. At its centre, within the drum, that plastic has a two inch circular hole cut in it and through this and to the side of the plastic falls the grain. A reservoir of grain remains above the plastic insert and the protruding ends of it can be rounded off to form something of a rain lip over the letter box. The plastic I use, and I get four from a standard square drum, is nine inches wide. The measurements I have given can be varied as long as there is a relationship between the distance of the plastic above the letter box, the size of the hole in the centre of it and the nature of the feed. Small tailings seem to fall well through the centre hole: a stiffer mixture might like more room. With these measurements, the feed will gradually reach to the top of the bottom lip of the letter-box. Some subsequent trials have shown that at such a level some grain will still be spilt by the birds and we shall be experimenting with the plastic insert placed even lower in the drums or more likely by raising the height of the bottom lip of the letter-box.

FAULTS. This type of feeder has several drawbacks which is an unfortunate thing to say of a feeder that has not yet been tested! I think the principal drawback, and that which accounts for our preference for the Owen Tickler, is that this feeder is not designed for cleanings. Cleanings will come through all right and a reservoir remain, but since they will consist of a large amount of straw and dross, the feed holes will quickly fill up with that when the accessible grain and seed has been pecked out. It would help if the bottom of the letter-box were to be made level with the floor of the drum; simple enough to arrange, but even then it seems unlikely that the birds would scratch out the dross to secure a fresh flow of food. The drum might be subject to interference from badgers and would be open to vermin, though that might be overcome. As the drums are of plastic, they would be liable to be blown about when empty unless secured. I hope to make some tests with this feeder in the coming season.

PROVIDING THE FOOD

Each pen has a forty gallon drum alongside it which contains a sack or two of grain for topping up purposes and at the same time that that is filled in readiness for the bird's arrival, several five gallon containers of water are left at the pen so that the water vessels can be regularly replenished. In a dry year particularly, there must be ample water available for birds fed on pellets or grain.

We have always been wasteful in our use of food and I think that that is a better description than to merely say 'extravagant'. My head keeper likes to scatter pellets generously round the pen when the birds arrive. He likes to scatter pellets and corn generously around the outside when the birds are released. The whole area is thick with corn. The birds, themselves, upon release, set out to empty the feeders by assiduously pecking at them. When the high conical heap around each feeder has sprouted well, my head keeper likes to get a shovel, run it round the heap and thrust the turf-like result into the hedge! He then fills the feeders again and scatters more corn. I remonstrate, but he says: 'Well, Geoff, the way I look at it, those birds are going to wander and when they are out in the middle of Poor Lot they will get bored and wonder what they can do and one little bright thing will say: "Why don't we all go back and hammer those feeders some more" and the rest of them will jump at the suggestion and if they are prepared to do that then I am prepared to keep filling the feeders for them'.

It may be interesting to note that for about 750 birds we have hitherto used well over two tons of wheat and twenty bags of pellets. Much of the food is wasted but, as my head keeper says, if it has served a purpose, all well and good. No doubt it enables a good deal of wild life to survive the winter and, indeed, to thrive. We are not unduly troubled by rooks and pigeon, possibly because we have powerful forces at hand to deal with any sudden descent! The actual cost of feeding as an expense of the Shoot is not excessive and, of course, the corn comes at a reasonable price from one or other of the farms whose owner has a Gun in the syndicate.

A CHANGE OF FOOD

Well, I have dwelt at some length on the subject of our past habits and I do not think it has been a waste of time to have done so. We may indeed find ourselves operating in the self-same way again in a couple of years time although I think the slit bottomed drum will be replaced by one of the others. What has happened to promote our present change has been, as I said earlier, our visit to Mr Keith Langdown's Shoot. On two matters he was specific and what he said made sense. It was never any good, he said, mixing pellets with the grain: the birds merely learnt to extract the pellets at the cost of removing all the grain from the container first. He got over the problem, he told us, by providing a more satisfactory food – tailings! When you examine a sack of good tailings you see at once that its contents: kibbled wheat, various weed seeds and chaff are eminently suited to partridge, but what is more, Mr Langdown assures us, faced with a tray of tailings and a tray of wheat, the birds will go for the tailings every time. That was his second point.

As a result of our visit we shall be using tailings this year. It will not make much difference to the food bill as I shall point out later. We are not so greatly concerned with cost: however, the point is, shall we have happier birds? That is something we have to find out.

To alter one's method of feeding in such a radical way is a great upset, calling for a lot of work and occasioning expense. First of all, slit drums are not much good when chaff is involved, nor are wire bottomed drums: both silt up quickly. Nor are birds likely to be helpful in pulling out the obstructing straw. A letter-box system can easily be designed to produce a steady supply of food and this can certainly be done by the two types I have described. Once again, however, the chaff and unpalatable seeds would remain at the bottom and the drums would cease to function. That is why we designed the Owen Feeder.

TAIL CORN

I am not sure that I am competent to write about tail corn. Indeed, the more I am told about it the more confused I become. During the war tail corn, or tailings, were a well known and staple product – the perquisite of the farmer, although he was not allowed to sell it. Indeed, one received thirty shillings for the several days' work helping when the thresher came and with it came the bonus of a sack of tailings for the chicken. Nowadays, tailings live an uneasy life, half way between being a luxury article and a nuisance. Those to whom tail corn, or tailings or cleanings, are a nuisance are happy for you to have them. For such farmers these tailings, full of straw and weed seed, are either to be burnt or to be sent straight to the pit. You are welcome to such as they may have but please do not spread any of those noxious seeds on their land, they say. Unfortunately, they can seldom supply a fixed quantity or guarantee any at all and what they have is likely to be green, that is to say, not artificially dried as the grain is. Never mind, they say, so and so up the road will have plenty. Mr So and So does have a ton or two guaranteed – at a price – but again it is probably green. You must bag it up and store it and since it is fifty per cent chopped straw, it is very bulky. When you store it, you should leave it on a shed floor where it will be well aired, yet dry: otherwise, it will heat up. Needless to say, you should use hessian bags! The economic price of wheat tailings, and it is wheat tailings that you want, is little less than that of wheat whole grain, for this is lovely stuff. 'Never worth that,' says your farmer friend, 'the first thing any farmer getting that much for his tailings would do is to get on the phone to his farmer friends and say, "Guess how much I've sold my tailings for?"' What choice have you, however? That sack of tailings, rich in weed seed, full of kibbled wheat and small ears is ideal for partridge. It is rich in protein, apparently, which means that it can be ground down as a valuable foodstuff. Here and there you may find someone who actually has dried tailings he is willing to sell and they will be worth the price. Perhaps the answer is to use such tailings as you can get hold of, green or otherwise, to hand feed the birds while keeping your drums filled with wheat. Again, you have to be careful how you spread weed seeds about. One feels it might be better to use kibbled or broken grain even in the drums. There are a lot of experiments still to be carried out in the feeding of the adult partridge. We do not think whole wheat grain is very successful: how much grain do you find in the crops of the birds which you shoot? They will certainly take the whole grain and I am sure that in captivity they can be maintained on it, but as an attraction to free birds, I feel it is of limited value. Unfortunately, you will have to go to the larger supplier to get kibbled wheat. Most farms used to have a hammer mill, which I think was the thing that used to do that sort of work, but most of those now remaining have important parts missing and the granary has a grinder which produces a rough flour to be turned into food pellets.

The small wheat grains sieved out at the dryer would probably be ideal for the purpose but apparently research has shown that these small grains have more value in a bread loaf than the larger grain and so they are not likely to be sifted out. The trouble is that when too much rubbish comes into the dryer, Charles sends a message across to Brian at the combine to that effect and he consequently makes an adjustment to the machine, the result of which is that more dross is ejected from the combine and onto the field than before. Then the blower at the granary has less work to do blowing out chaff and fewer siftings are produced.

Nor is it just the problem that fewer cleanings are produced. If your season has been a bad one, then it is likely that the whole crop will be sold as feed wheat and, in that case, the cleaning need be minimal – it will all be ground down to feed animals: so you cannot win. Even the thought that perhaps a ton or two of hard won green cleanings might be put through the dryer at an economical price was scotched by my farmer friend who tells me that his machinery cannot economically deal with less than fifteen tons at a time.

Perhaps you had better get in touch with one of the large co-operatives and see what they have for sale if you want to try your hand at tailings. It is probably not so important whether they are dried or green. Most will be used within ten weeks of delivery. I still feel that a nice mix of kibbled wheat oats and a few other grains should be tried. If your farmer landlord is supplying your needs you will have to put up with whatever he has to give you and may consider yourself very lucky to be so provided whatever it is because a number of problems such as storage will be eliminated. Whatever you end up with see that the farmer has ready access to the place of storage and knows the manner of feedings. He can then make clear at once whether he has any reservation as to its use or the manner of its use on his land. It may be that pelleted seed spread by the family horse has made him nervous and, although I may be condemned by many for saying so, not every farmer is aware that birds have gizzards and that they grind their corn leaving no trail of weeds behind.

WATERING

For watering we use plastic drums cut longitudinally. Outside the pens, these are fine, except that they are apt to be white and stand out in consequence. Inside the pens, they are something of a failure as far as I am concerned. They have to be cleaned for each intake and in a matter of hours seem to be filthy again. Placing bricks in them is a help, but it is not the answer to the problem. I think the use of small automatic plastic water containers would be best but there is a strong feeling on a well-motivated Shoot against buying what might be improvised. I should like to get some small tyres for use inside the pens and larger ones for outside. Cut in half, I think that these would provide a discreet and reasonably unfouled supply of water. So far, I regret to admit, I have not found an efficient method of cutting tyres. In the meantime, by placing the existing half drums inside black plastic dustbin liners, or green plastic garden sacks, we shall render them less obvious.

WINTER FEEDING

The subject of winter feeding is one which really deserves its own chapter, save that not enough is known about it to fill more than a line or two. I like Mr Noel M. Sedgwick's account of feeding partridge in his book *The Young Shot*. Apparently, in those days (not so long ago) a few handfuls of wheat thrown on the ground towards the end of the season, and one did not shoot much past November, prevented the birds straying away towards the arable! He almost speaks of it as though it were cheating! But in those days, they managed to shoot 150 brace on his downland without any of the trouble described in this book.

What one would like to do is not only to feed into the spring, but to provide something for the young birds through June and July. At least science, which has so upset the aphid, has provided the right food for young birds. What we lack is some reliable means of getting this to the very small beaks of the wild nestlings. 'In any case, its putting the cart before the horse', I hear you say. In one of those books touching on partridge, *Syndicate Shooting*, F. G. Standfield speaks of a man who used to put the odd pitch fork of dung near known nests so that there might be a source of food nearby for the young birds. That man was a true pioneer! Perhaps something can be put under our winter feed shelters that will give these small birds strength to survive in a hard world. Small blocks of soluble food around the Shoot to be pecked at perhaps? 'Why not umbrellas?' you will ask, and of course I know that food is only a part of the problem. Obviously, these are the thoughts of a novice: nevertheless, the problems of rearing partridge in captivity have been largely surmounted. Perhaps this next step will be taken and healthy chicks once more survive in the wild.

In the past, our winter feeding has been haphazard. Food has been left in the feeders to be taken by all and sundry, to be pecked out onto the ground by the partridge there, to shoot out and waste and, worst of all, to shoot within the slits of the drums while that within the drum itself went mouldy. This winter has been one of experiment with different types of feeders but the weather has been so mild that the birds have not shown the interest that a hard winter would induce. Since we are now determined to use the Owen Tickler next year, it has been necessary to design shelters for those and with considerable effort we are erecting shelters for over fifty feeders. These consist of a short length of corrugated iron run from each side of a rail supported by two posts: the drum hangs from the rail and the whole becomes a tent-like stucture. In order to ensure all round visibility and approach, the ends of the corrugated iron are held six inches off the ground by pegs. For a pen with a minimum of four feeders, that means sixteen small supporting pegs alone and experience teaches us that we may have been a little over elaborate here! Probably, there is no need to elevate the bottom of the corrugated iron inside the pens: they could be set into the ground.

As a consequence of the erection of these feeders, we hope that winter feeding will be very simple. Of course, there is a riot of possibilities and particularly by using the hosepipe type of feeder, the building of a shelter can be greatly simplified. Inside the pens, the pipe might be led through or down the side of the existing shelter, while outside it might be led through a 2 ft 6 in square section of corrugated iron set at a slight angle on four one foot high pegs. Food left in the release pens in any type of sheltered feeder will be protected from the elements, secure from badgers as the birds themselves are from foxes and it will be much less available to corvids.

THE RELEASE

> Stay, stay at home, my heart, and rest;
> Home keeping hearts are happiest,
> For those that wander they know not where
> Are full of trouble and full of care;
> To stay at home is best.
> Weary and homesick and distressed,
> They wander east, they wander west,
> And are baffled and beaten and blown about
> By the winds of the wilderness of doubt;
> To stay at home is best.
> *Stay at home*, H. W. Longfellow

We would like to start by keeping our birds in the pen for a week and then releasing a few at a time over the next week or two. In the chapter on timing I explain how difficult it is to find time for this. We like to leave three or more in each pen to act as 'callers', that is to say, birds which will anchor down those birds already released to this particular territory, entertain passing birds generally and join their voices to those of the released birds in reply to distant chatter from other pens.

Basically, the object of releasing a few at a time is said to be to bunch the birds up into artificial and manageable coveys. In my experience of Red-legs on our land, that does not work at all. The coveys all join up in the early days and disperse in a very haphazard fashion, I feel sure, later. This does not matter as long as you are not driving them immediately from the pens to the Guns and even if the final pen is near the brow above the Guns, as in one of our drives, there is generally a certain amount of rough cover into which the birds will run before their final flight and from this cover they will generally take off in ones and twos. Not so the Greys, of course, each lot of these needs its own patch and what you release there will generally become the covey. No, the real effect of staggered release is the holding power that the birds left in the pen exert on those released and, eventually, that the majority which has been released, exercises on the minority now joining it outside.

The recommended method of releasing birds is to leak a few out of the pophole but on our bare ground that is unthinkable. If we opened our popholes, the birds that ran out would fly and fly and fly. Since we cannot use the pophole method, our practice used to be to catch the birds up by hand as suggested for Red-legs by the Game Conservancy. We do still use the direct pophole method with our Greys on roots, but that is a very different matter and they have generally been talking to their wild mates for a long time. For some reason, we are able to give them two or three weeks before their release – well, I know very well why. It is because they are in a part of the farm where there is no great likelihood of outside interference and neither is there any great hurry to move them on to make room for other birds.

It was a very hard business the first time I released birds by hand and so it was the second time. My height makes jumping around five foot pens very difficult. It is always raining when one releases in such circumstances so one is jumping around with a fair amount of gear on. For catching up the birds, I tried various nets with mixed success, even one of hessian. I found stiff garden netting best. Having caught up half the number to be released, if one could hold such a number, one took them out gingerly and put them on their sides very gently under the thick grass of a hedge. Sometimes we had to scatter straw along the barren hedge side in order to provide some cover to put the birds in. Then back for the second half of the release, back aching, these to be put down in the same way in another patch of grass on the other side of the pen so as not to disturb the first set. After their panic as they were caught, sometimes injured in the course of their blind dashes to avoid capture, the birds would lie quietly in the grass if one was lucky. Sometimes, one would get up and fly, sometimes two. Often, when it was two, the disturbance would cause the rest of that release to take off with them flying fast and far, off into the next valley. As far as we were concerned, we did not expect them back. Perhaps some came back, perhaps not, their next flight, if disturbed again, would take them well beyond our boundaries. The release, therefore was and is a vital part of partridge management. Of course, we spared no pains and we became expert at it.

I wanted my head keeper to put a small wire enclosure in the corner of the pens, something that would normally be open and with which the birds would not be concerned but in which the selected number could be trapped without trauma and from which they could be released in our usual way or perhaps via the adjoining pophole. I had in mind for this latter purpose placing a length of large mesh chicken wire horizontally on one foot high pegs outside the pophole under which the grass would grow thickly giving a dense cover. Through this, the birds would struggle and, no doubt, linger at the time of release. At any rate, they would not be able to fly in the first moments of freedom. I used a similar scheme this year where a single pen was sited near a wall and this worked very well with me, though not so well with a colleague who released there. My experience is that the longer the birds are penned, the less likely they are to fly but so often one has to release earlier than one would wish.

To my pleasure, I found that on setting up the pens this year on a Shoot from which we had been absent for two years, my head keeper had designed the double pen system complete with pophole between pens and with anti-fox grids through which the birds are finally released. I think this is the crowning achievement of his ten years as an amateur keeper on a partridge manor. The double pen allows for endless possibilities – all simple, none of them backbreaking and all leaving the poults unconcerned. An additional and perhaps obvious use of the release pen is as a catcher at the end of the season. All that is required is the addition of a simple mesh funnel.

The new double pen is shown in the illustration on page 32. The birds having been penned in one part of the pen, the person releasing them first of all sees that the plywood board is securely fixed over the fox grids. Then he opens the pophole between the pens and prepares to count out the number of birds he wishes to release as they enter the second pen. Of course, they do no such thing: they peer and consider and walk around their parent pen, obviously hoping to find a hole in the wire through which they may obtain their freedom. Sometimes, several go through the exit and stand blocking it, often several return. When they do at last start to go, their exit quickly becomes a rout. This is quite all right if the person releasing is unhurried and perhaps a contemplative pipe smoker, but for others it may be tedious. If time is short then the initial procedure may be gone through the day before or even the day before that. When the time comes to release them the birds will run knowledgeably from one pen to another and can be released from whichever is convenient or has at that time the right number of birds in it. Whichever you do, once you have the required number of birds in the section from which you are going to release them, you simply close the pophole between the pens, remove the cover from in front of the fox grids, and walk away. It gives great pleasure when one sees all or most of the birds back inside the release section the next morning and, in some cases, it will be obvious that they have been jugging there secure from the larger vermin but at liberty. Over the days, we found the number remaining in dwindled and varied but often there

Sunbathing on a shelter prior to release

would be seven or eight birds in a release section particularly when the holding section had a fresh batch of birds in. On shoot days, we go round and as the lodgers rapidly run out we close their entry for the time being.

Of our intention to make the two parts of the double pen interchangeable, I have spoken elsewhere; also, of our hopes that in hard times after the season is over, the birds will return to these fox proof quarters for the grain which will be left dry and available there under the shelters. In the chapter on timing I have dealt with the intervals between release in greater detail.

DRIVING PARTRIDGE

> The first physicians by debauch were made;
> Excess began, and sloth sustains the trade.
> By chase our long liv'd fathers earn'd their food;
> Toil strung the nerves, and purifi'd the blood;
> But we their sons, a pamper'd race of men,
> Are dwindled down to threescore years and ten,
> Better to hunt in fields for health unbought,
> Than fee the doctor for a nauseous draught,
> The wise for cure on exercise depend;
> God never made His work for man to mend.
>
> John Dryden

The text books lay down a number of rules for driving partridge and basically they seem to be these:
1. Partridge should be driven towards known cover – into the roots, if you like, and thence over the Guns.
2. The birds will not be found in the roots or other thick cover when it is damp and wet.
3. Partridge must be driven with the wind.

Now I will deal with each of these three rules separately but I will make it clear that these are not rules for us. The king of driven partridge is the Red-leg: we release a vast majority of Red-legs. For Red-legs, rules 1, 2 and 3 are not absolute.

To these rules we may add for consideration the following:
4. Partridge will fly towards their release pens.
5. Partridge will fly towards the release pens and the communities of their fellows.

1. Partridge should be driven towards known cover

It is important to emphasize here that we are dealing with released Red-legs rather than with Greys. At the same time, we do have some natural or wild coveys of Red-legs and of Greys and we do release a few Greys. This rule was much more important in the old days: they were the days of the wild Grey partridge. All things being equal, that bird will make for cover, certainly where good roots are available – heavy kale is no good. This was the most important rule in the days when the birds were walked up because it is only when they are in cover that the Greys will lie close and rise within range of a walking Gun. Even Red-legs will sometimes stop running in cover!

If you had lots of nice tussocky fields, some rough stubbles and roots down in the valley all dotted about with coveys of Greys, it would be a fine thing to blank in the valley edges, field after field, picking up a covey here and a covey there, watching them sail down into the roots, and I use the word in a wide sense to include clover and cover crops generally, there to provide a superb drive when all was complete. I suppose that you might do much of this blanking in before the Guns assemble. On our own Shoot we should be tempted to shoot the birds on their way to the cover – but of course that is exactly the way it would have been done with a number of walking Guns in the old days! Suffice it to say that had you fields enough and cover enough then you could walk or drive your birds to cover and thence walk or drive them.

In short then, rule 1, first brought about in the course of walking up partridge and latterly applied by way of advice where birds are driven, applies primarily to the Grey partridge, the English bird. The Red-leg, once deemed a nuisance on a Shoot because of its habit of running on, has been accepted by many modern writers as something that may well join in the fun without any proper consideration for its little ways. The truth is, that far from being an adjunct to the sport of driven partridge shooting, on Shoots where the birds are mainly released and on downland Shoots, certainly, the Red-leg is the important bird and it is not appropriate to quote the rule that applies to Greys and to expect one to fit the Red-leg into the pattern as well as one may. Our intensive farming system with its vast areas of plough, little cover and little intimacy, is designed for the Red-leg and not the Grey. A modern partridge Shoot can put down a thousand Red-legs and expect to enjoy a modest success, whereas on the same land two thousand Greys could prove a complete disaster. It is important to remember that the art of driving Red-legs is altogether different from the art of driving Greys.

On our own Shoot we have an overwhelming majority of Red-legs but sufficient Greys for such roots as we expect to have. A few Greys among Red-legs will run with the majority and can be brought over the Guns despite a lack of cover. On their own and once in the majority, the Greys will go straight up into the air: all right for your tussocky field, all right for well-hedged country and all right if you are going to watch them down into the roots and take them from there but not much good over a lot of modern farmland.

So we run our Red-legs and fly our Greys and the two things are quite different and you are entitled to ask: 'Well! How do you do it then?' So let us wander away from rule number one for a while.

Our first requirement is for a well disciplined team of beaters at least half of whom know the land like the back of their hands. It is important that at the start of each drive the keeper should put the plan of action quite clearly to all the beaters. They should know the line of advance, the picking up points, as it were, and the place of discharge – that, as I explain later, may vary considerably with the wind. They should be lined up without haste in the shape of a horse shoe, a flanker on each side. The flanker should be at least a hundred yards in front of the beating line because we expect our Red-legs to run on a considerable distance ahead. The flanker is not given his flag as a mark of distinction nor as a casual amusement: it is to be rolled up and tucked into his side until the moment comes for its proper use. When birds flush and head towards him, he will unroll and crack his flag (he will be expected to do it quicker than that!) It is that sudden flash of colour and the crack that will turn the birds back to the path of duty. It is for that emphasis that the flag is kept rolled up and out of sight until it is needed. We use a colour called 'Dayglow Orange' which is sold by the Game Conservancy and selected by them as the most surprising colour that a partridge could expect to see. Often, the flanker will be walking a hedge line and will see a covey of Red-legs running along in front of him. It is his job then to jump the hedge regardless of the damage he may do to the barbed wire and run and flank those birds, using the flag if necessary, flanking them back into the centre of the drive. There may be an exception when more flags are distributed along the line to be waved and cracked as the beaters progress in an effort to get the birds to go against the wind.

Our aim then, with our own Red-legs, a few Greys among them we pray, is to run or fly them to the end of our drive keeping them in the centre of our line (impossible, of course) – or to a line of plough if that has been drawn out for us – and then at the end of the drive to tip them slowly but steadily, over the brow of the hill above the waiting Guns. We may have a strip of cover, mustard perhaps, at this point and the birds can be driven slowly from it. In favourable circumstances, the beaters will halt twenty yards from such a flushing point and the head keeper and his dog or trusted lieutenant slowly walk the cover from end to end. It is true that we do like a flushing point if we can get it. The

Nicely over. From a photograph by Paul Middleton

birds will rise more steadily from this so to some extent you may say that we do drive to cover but a flushing point is not quite the same thing as a field of roots. We can get much the same effect by using a wall or a hedge which bounds a hillside. With any luck and some co-operation from the farmer, the wall will have a good verge of rough grass and perhaps bramble and what an asset that can be: offering shelter from sun and rain, a sunning place when it is windy or a place of refuge when the vermin man comes round. Unfortunately, it may also be a highway for other traffic! Such a wall can form a flushing point and when the birds have been run into it, then, ever so carefully, they can be pressed until, in small groups, they sail up and journey over the valley. Perhaps you can arrange for a strip of kale to be planted on a three year basis alongside the wall?

To summarise rule number 1 then, one has to say Red-legs do not need cover in the form of a field of roots or clover or something of that sort, but if one is lucky enough to have such cover, then adjoining fields will be blanked into it and the birds driven from there. Such fields are primarily the flushing points for the Greys. Since our hills are generally bare of cover, the Greys oblige by flying great distances almost as soon as the beaters enter their particular field and, if you are lucky, fly over the Guns to give them a taste of the impossible to come and to punish them for not being alert. The Red-legs are run and they do like a flushing point though it may only be a hedge, wall or line of mustard.

2. The birds will not be found in the roots or other thick cover when it is damp and wet

It is true of course that the birds are not keen on wet cover: in fact Red-legs dislike it even more than the Greys do, but the Red-legs are not really cover birds. One can understand this business about wet cover: its a very nasty place for anyone to be and as an occasional beater, I speak with some feeling. If it is thick kale you probably will never have many birds in it, that is to say, if it is a field of kale, a strip of kale is a very good thing. We are very lucky as we tend to get a field with rows of swedes alternating with strips of kale which provide good cover and good drying areas. Even when we only have swedes those roots tend to hold the Greys. The trouble is that there are not many places for the Greys to go and those who have adopted the swedes as the place of their choice will be there, wet or fine. If it is wet then the birds are likely to be around the edges or under a boundary wall but it is there

Breaking away. *Paul Middleton*

that they will be and when the drive commences it is from the roots that they will rise. That does not mean that there will be no Greys in the stubbles. They will be there, in the mustard or slipping over the brow just as those that belong to the roots will be there. You may get more in one place than the other depending on the weather. Of course, you cannot be dogmatic about partridge and there is a proviso to everything. If the foxes have held a convention in your roots the night before you shoot, then you will be puzzled. Certainly, you hope to get a few wandering Red-legs from the roots although you seldom find the hundred or more you believe to be missing but the truth of the matter is that the roots are a valuable area of the Shoot and you are going to beat the roots whether you quote rule 2 or not: so I suppose you may as well forget it. Before I leave that rule it is relevant to point out that our roots generally offer us hedgerow shooting which is not our metier – our hedges are not good ones and do not offer good stands as our hillsides do. Furthermore, our roots are, as chance has it, rather on the extremity of our Shoot so that we are generally more interested in driving birds from the roots back into the centre of the Shoot than filling up the roots from the centre as rule 1 would have it.

3. Partridge must be driven with the wind

Now rule number 3 is much more relevant for us and is one that must always be at the back of the downland shooter's mind. It is odd, come to think of it, that we drive from all points of the compass though not often from the south. Every Shoot has a prevailing wind and that is the thing to take into account. At the same time, if you can ease a couple of coveys up to the edge of a steep slope bounded by some feature, hedge or kale strip perhaps, and tip them over the edge then they are likely to give shooting to those below whatever, within reason, the weather may be. We start our first drive from the extreme north picking up a few birds here and a few birds there. We find a few at the northernmost pen, a few more at the three middle pens and they join with those in the vicinity of the bottom or southernmost pen. Then they are all pushed over the edge of the escarpment. I suppose a very strong southerly wind would pose problems and they might blow back on us but the wind is generally westerly and the birds sweep over and travel the contours with the wind. The stronger the wind, the further to the east we place our line of Guns. The stronger the wind, the more delicate must the beating be. The slightest haste, a dog too far forward, and the birds will rise on

The keeper demonstrates – or is it a dance? *Paul Middleton*

the wind and sweep away to the east and that will be the risk throughout the whole long drive. If you can push the birds one way against a modest wind, they will certainly provide a fine return drive.

Not only will we swing our Guns to catch the drift of the birds when there is a wind but we shall align the beaters to drive the birds rather into the wind so that, taking off, as we hope, one at a time, they will swing down the line of Guns. We will make the Guns aware of our intentions so that the less fortunate will not feel that they have been robbed of their sport by some careless or deliberate ploy of the beating team.

In my penultimate paragraph I have used the expression 'strong wind' a little loosely. I do not really mean a strong wind on the Beaufort scale or a force six or seven. I mean a strong wind relevant to driving Red-legs. Now your young Red-leg, not long released, is a delicate bird in a wind. He will run so far but inevitably end up by veering to one side or to another. Later in the season he will fly more strongly: so it is not only a question of what is a strong wind. The question is: 'How strong are the birds?' Recently my head keeper told me his contingency plans for the first drive, which is the long north to south drive which I have already described, in the event of a strong wind. One would expect the difficult wind to be a south-easterly one. First of all the Guns would be asked to wait at an accessible spot at the centre of this long drive and at the easterly side of it. They would be asked to wait quietly there and my head keeper anticipates that ten Guns, lighting cigars, passing the bottle round, calling their dogs to heel and conversing in loud whispers would generate just the right amount of noise to keep the birds to the west side of the drive. Upon the beating line, coming parallel to the Guns and passing on, the Guns would line up behind them. There is a very suitable cross hedge here running the width of the drive. The beaters would proceed slowly and carefully up the sheltered incline which runs from the hedge with as many birds as possible in front of them. At the crest from which the birds would normally be driven onto the edge of the escarpment and over the waiting Guns the full force of the 'strong' wind would be felt. In ones and twos the birds would lift, swing over the beaters and speed across the waiting Guns two hundred yards or more back. Well, we all have our dreams but it is just as well to dream up contingency plans while you are about it.

I suppose I have not yet experienced a gale but one accepts that no reared bird is going to be driven against a gale. That is something I think we shall have to make a rule about when we come to it. I am sure that the rule ought to be to cancel the Shoot straight away if there is doubt. It is not so much a question of whether one can get the birds over the Guns but of where the birds are going to end up when driven from our heights with a stiff breeze behind them. Of course, your Guns are busy men and it is impossible at that stage in the season to arrange a fresh date that will suit more than half of them. Furthermore, they have given up valuable time and may not be able to spare more. You are concerned that they have paid dearly for a day's sport. In fact, they have paid for a masterpiece and however much they have paid they must not endanger it in any way: the viewing can wait. The modest sum laid out for an inestimable privilege can carry no weight in your deliberation. I am sure that shoots should be cancelled more often. Perhaps the rule should be that every list of shooting days should have at least one spare day added so that there need be no arranging, no arguing if a set day proves inhospitable.

Having achieved our first drive, whether we put a good head of birds over the Guns or not, we have certainly stirred up all the birds down the centre of the Shoot. Most, it is true, will have gone eastwards and it is from the north and the east that our next drive commences. This is a very wide drive but we are driving birds into the centre of the Shoot as well as down a steep slope over the Guns. If the wind is westerly, then we shall be driving into it: again, the birds will take off into the wind.

This time, some of them will have it in mind to return to the centre of the Shoot whence they came and this may influence others to commence their flight forward into such wind as there may be. When the wind hits them they will swerve but the Guns below are in a crescent formation and are not likely to be robbed of their sport although the tally may be reduced. We may then drive the roots from the western side of the Shoot and here the birds will fly fast and straight if there is a wind, back to the centre of the Shoot.

An east wind will have much the same effect for us, save that fast birds from the roots will be replaced by fast birds from our eastern hill and we shall now debate the direction of our drive from the roots which being usually hedge bound allows us that choice although we much prefer to drive towards the centre of the Shoot. One has to experiment: one of our drives this year will be northwards across an east to west valley so we shall have to see what the various winds do to this. Most days, the wind is not strong enough to affect the settled drives. When it is, then must the keeper and the captain of the Guns confer. Far more damning is heavy rain leaving one uncertain whether to go on; or the mists to which we are rather more subject and which are equally uncertain as to their comings and goings. For us the wind and the weather generally are variables which must be taken into acocunt on the day.

4. and 5.   Partridge will fly towards their release pens or the pens and communities of their fellows

The most important factor in settling the drives is the site of the various release pens and these have been sited so as to provide the best drives. They have been sited so as to provide a holding power at a point which is a suitable distance from the point at which the birds, with or without released birds from other pens and in company with odd coveys, will be put over the Guns. In this scheme of things, the wind has already been taken into account. The rule for released birds is that they may be driven from a release area which contains sufficient calling power in the shape of caller birds left in the pens to bring them back home again after the drive. They may be driven from a release area which they have adopted as their home territory and to which they will have an urge to return when it is safe for them to do so. Birds will also drive towards other release areas where they have established communication with the inhabitants. Thus you may take in a number of pens on your drive collecting odds and ends from the vicinity of each. One must add a proviso to these rules and that is that the release sites must represent a secure haven and the management of the birds there must have been good. That is why a quiet release is so important: if the birds have been harried at the pen by a fox or dog, then they will quickly sever their connection with that site.

Other words of wisdom in respect of the driving of partridge I have dropped in the chapter 'Keepers and Beaters'. It is sufficient now if I merely emphasize the need for silence from man and dog. The need for the keeper to be informed by means of hand signals passed from one to another of the location of the various coveys picked up so that again by signal he may stop or advance part of the line.

PLACING THE GUNS

It is said that Guns under low hedges should stand well into them to conceal themselves as well as they may from oncoming birds. Where the hedge is high enough then it is said that the Gun should stand some twenty-five yards back from it in order to take a reasonable shot as the birds break over. It is said that on open ground, as I suppose is constituted by our hillside stands, some sort of butt or screen should be constructed. Such a butt could be made of sheep hurdles or sheep netting but would at once have the disadvantage of confining the Gun to a set place. We do not find it necessary to provide a butt although I can imagine that it might be helpful in some places. A more advanced suggestion which would certainly not suit us is that the Gun might be given a roll of hessian fixed to four six foot bamboo canes to stick up at his chosen spot.

If you like the idea of four bamboo canes and a roll of hessian, and this will reduce the large number of butts otherwise to be provided, then I hope that you will have the sense to get the captain of the Guns to hand them round. The recriminations likely to follow such largesse from Guns who have spent their time trying to get bamboo canes into our hillsides after a half a day's dry weather, or who have pursued their cover down a hillside in the course of a drive could be quite demoralising! No doubt down where the valley sheep are fatter the rich soil will more readily accept a cane. My own experience is limited to pigeon hides and I can be emphatic that bamboo canes in our soil generally lead to disappointment.

Apart from stands or hides made of bamboo and hessian (and I only question these) all these observations as to the placing of Guns have merit, but I find that the more reliable their source the more likely they are to be chiefly related to pre-release days. Thus I would want my hurdles placed in position at least by the time my first birds were to be released. If they were placed out in advance then I would not mind moving them about on the morning of the Shoot to take into account the strength of the wind – or rather I would not mind someone else doing it! It would represent quite a lot of work and I think you would have to have quite a lot of partridge going over the Guns to justify such work.

Yes, it is good to stand up to a low hedge and away from a high hedge. There are occasions, however, when one may be better off in front of a low hedge. Perhaps one will be hardly more visible in front than when behind and the benefit of being in front will be that the birds, thinking to land in the hedge as they will after a fairly long approach, will think twice on seeing the Gun and brace themselves to fly higher or away to one side giving you or your neighbour a far more sporting shot and saving themselves from the unromantic end which a slow flip over the hedge might have led to! Remember, we are not in the lush lands of the small fields and the thick hedge! Of course you will have to try this out. If the coveys see the line of Guns from afar and have time to swing away out of range then this trick will not be for you. Eight or ten standing Guns make a very long line and if you are driving large fields you may find that it works.

Exactly the same thing may be said for the high hedge. Again I tend to refer to the sort of country where a high hedge bounds a forty acre field and rather than fly over it the birds are set to land in it. It is those birds that are put up early in the drive and thus have enjoyed a fairly long flight who see the hedge before them and instead of landing in the field glide on a low plane towards the known cover of the hedge. Try putting the Guns in front: the line as a whole will probably merge fairly well with the hedge. The one or two birds approaching any one Gun will rise fast and swerve, offering good shooting.

GENERALLY

You will find on the first Shoot that the reared birds stick fairly tightly to the ground but after a couple of Shoots have been held all become wild, demanding great caution and patience from the beaters. Unlike the pheasant which loses its wind quite quickly, the partridge can be driven over the Guns and then returned: it will fly as well the second time as the first. This is very important because it is convenient to return the birds to the centre of the Shoot before the end of the day and also because the birds in the return flight are far more likely to fly singly or in pairs. In this fashion the gun will have a better chance and the shooting will be more general and effective. Often on the first drive when there is little or no cover from which to flush the birds they will pack and fly the Guns in one great untouched flight. A return journey will restore the balance.

A useful tip is for the keeper to try to approach the pens each day from the direction which will be taken by the beaters on a shooting day. Before long the birds will be running on in the direction the drive will eventually take at the first hint of the keeper's arrival. If something of a point can be made of this as from, say, the second week of release then not only will the birds go further and further as they become wilder but they will also return more quickly as they get to know the country and it is the return of the birds after each shoot or indeed disturbance that we are so keen to see.

THE SECOND SYNDICATE

> There was a young lady of Niger
> Who went out with a smile on a tiger;
> They came back from the ride
> With the lady inside
> And the smile on the face of the tiger
>
>   Anon.

Most of the beaters on our Shoot come from two local industries as far removed from country matters as can be. Some, in common employment with my head keeper had no real connection with the countryside; others had their own sporting interests: rabbits, pigeon, duck perhaps. Now they were drawn into the work of a partridge Shoot and that of a nearby pheasant Shoot: the attraction at first was no doubt the novelty. They worked hard, keeping a tight rein on their tongues, lining up as they were directed, running a little to the left when urged to do so and halting in line when the signal was given. Someone said to me on the pheasant Shoot, 'How on earth does Bob (the Shoot owner) manage to get fifteen or sixteen beaters here every time?' There were small rewards: in lieu of payment there would be one or two beaters' shoots on the two undertakings, a few pigeon when they came onto the stubbles and rabbits. Sometimes enough rabbits for the whole team to have a grand day divided into small parties each with a few ferrets.

Having found by virtue of a few beaters' shoots that the art of shooting driven partridge or pheasant was an elusive art and that their own performance was exactly that which, had they not been so disciplined, they might have been tempted to criticise in some of the Guns on formal shoots; they could not help but be infused with the desire to do more, to achieve success – in short, to obtain some regular shooting.

It is this sort of person, no doubt, who writes to the sporting press from time to time asking how they can obtain sporting rights at a reasonable price. Of course if you want to spend time racing motor cars or paragliding or even sailing there is a price to pay and the question these young men seem to be asking or need to ask is: how can they avoid payment? The answer that the sporting press usually gives them is a good one. It is that they should become beaters. At any rate, keep beating is what our lads did.

My head keeper was well aware of the feelings and needs of his team of beaters and did what he could to satisfy them but it was very apparent that their real need was for a Shoot of their own, and one which would fill their requirements as to location and price was not an easy thing to find.

The relationship between part-time keeper, beaters and the owner of the partridge Shoot became a very close one and indeed, the farmer, who was busy enough, was able to leave so much in the hands of his regular team that he had little difficulty in the course of discussion in taking the decision to hand the Shoot over to a syndicate of the beaters.

The idea was to put down a greater number of birds and to provide three days of first class shooting for paying Guns who were to be known as the 'first syndicate'. Then the beaters, who were to be known as the 'second syndicate' were to put down such further birds as they wished and have the subsequent shooting. In effect, by putting down sufficient birds to ensure even shooting and a resultant large surplus after the last shoot of the first syndicate, the second syndicate took over a Shoot in its prime, as it were. The birds which they added, not only ensured even shooting on their own days but as a necessary concommitment, provided a good breeding stock for the land. For his part the farmer received two free Guns in the first syndicate.

The advantages were quickly apparent: the farmer knew that any suggestions he made would be received with interest, he had absolutely no worries of planning, organisation or finance and he still had a de facto control. The beating and the keepering were firmly taken care of and the beater's shoot became a thing of the past. Instead following on the last shoot by the first syndicate two or three hundred more birds were put in the pens acting as a powerful draw for all the birds released earlier, providing great holding power, and the second syndicate took its turn.

We have certain conventions which should ensure that the ground is well managed and not overshot. We do not, for instance, release any Greys at the final release because of the late season. Nor do we reckon to shoot any partridge, certainly not Greys, after the 31 December. We do not regard ourselves as finished at the end of the year because our days may be part partridge and part pheasant or either and our season is also extended by beaters' shoots elsewhere.

The second syndicate is governed by the Shoot organiser: my head keeper. All are answerable to him. The yellow card which each member displays in his car carries the Shoot organiser's telephone number and it is to him that any complaints, or more likely cries for help, are sent. The card is displayed so that any landowner or farm worker will see at a glance that the car driver is an authorised person. The members are expected to act responsibly, keeping an eye open for straying cattle and matters that will interest the farmer. Nor do they exercise their rights in any haphazard fashion. Most of the shooting results from the farmer reporting pigeon or rabbit damage and the Shoot organiser will ring round to get a Gun in place. A report detailing the events of the day will generally be made – by way of an informal telephone call. It would be irritating otherwise to creep round on a bird releasing exercise to find someone sitting in a hide between two pens blasting away at pigeon. That is a far fetched example but the same applies to my little pheasant wood where I do not expect to see anyone.

The remaining Guns of the first syndicate are let out at a modest sum to much the same body of sportsmen who shot here before. The money received is not sufficient to run the Shoot as it is run but the subscription of the members of the second syndicate helps pay for the original stocking as it pays for such further birds as they decide to put down for themselves. In fact they are also able to put a few pheasant down on adjoining land in order to spread their own shooting.

The Guns of the first syndicate look after themselves under the captaincy of the farmer with very few rules save that they must respect the pheasants. The rule is that they must not shoot a pheasant unless it is a really good one, that is to say, almost out of sight!

Nor has this been all to come from our machinations because the owner of adjoining land when approached with the usual seasonal offering of a brace of well prepared birds, and they are much better dealt with in this way than any other, on being asked for the usual licence to stand on his ground from time to time, suggested that the second syndicate now take on his land. Hitherto he had let a number of people use guns on his land but his rabbits had multiplied and indeed I think there had been some embarrassment when one or two of his licensees had wandered from his land and onto more productive soil! Now the syndicate have another thousand acres at their disposal and we shall have a pen and a potentially good drive there this year. If all goes well we shall be able to use our new land to relieve the centre of our existing Shoot.

The second syndicate now have a very large area of land at their disposal. None of it is good pheasant country, what game comes from it must be put there in the first place and protected but the intensive feeding system in use for the partridge, spread out as it is, is attractive to

Venison butties again! *Paul Middleton*

pheasant. Thus they tend to frequent the rather bare hedges of our partridge country and to breed there. The few strips of kale we shall have will provide an added attraction.

There are advantages all round in running a syndicate in the way we do. The first one no doubt is that of cost but not least among them is the sense of comradeship which develops among the members. There is always something amusing on the go. One remembers the time when a member was trying out an old hammer gun as a number of us were decoying pigeon on laid corn. Both barrels went off at once. The pigeon died but we spent a few minutes looking for a set of teeth! There was a day when the head keeper took possession of a roe deer, the victim of a traffic accident, in circumstances where the ownership could be said to have rightly devolved in the club rather than on an individual. Andy was determined to get a joint, something he felt was owing to him, and he would not let the matter alone. My head keeper could not take out a sandwich without reference being made to its contents. Eventually he parleyed saying that of course there was a joint in the freezer for Andy and that he should come and collect it that night. When Mrs Andy opened the parcel that night she found to her hysterical surprise that it contained half a pig's head. Nor would that have mattered so much but that, left thawing in the kitchen overnight, it proved an irresistible temptation to the spaniel who ate well but not wisely, to the detriment of floor coverings everywhere. Andy's absolute fury was shattered when he learnt that he had simply taken the wrong parcel. To continue the history to the second parcel he received would be to make a long story!

Such a syndicate as we run has advantages too over the privately owned Shoot. Our beating was always done freely but now a good deal of work is done which no Shoot owner would expect Guns or beaters to do. The Shoot owner knows that the odd acre of kale is a loss to the farm. He may have to sweeten his partners to get it sown. When the farm workers are called upon to extend the pheasant pen there is an understandable reluctance to incorporate more good land than is strictly necessary. The syndicate on the other hand, one such as ours at any rate, can look at its finances and plan its needs accordingly. It may decide that an extra ten pounds per member will buy an acre of kale and proceed to buy it. This would probably not be of such value if the landlord did not shoot but ours does and if he gets an economic return from his land then he is prepared to put hard work into providing kale or even a line of fencing. He has every incentive because in such circumstances it becomes a matter of business.

I do not suppose that such opportunities as the second syndicate have had are easily come by nor is there always the right organiser or the right farmer but it does seem that this is a good practical example of the good that may come of beating.

OF DOGS AND PICKERS-UP

> So all day long the noise of battle roll'd
> Among the mountains by the winter sea
> *Morte d'Arthur*, Tennyson

It is only recently that I have emerged from the chrysalis of a rabbiting man to the status of a game person. I still enjoy my rabbiting but the days when two of us wandered around with guns and a couple of dogs are over. Those dogs used to attend at once upon the report of a gun yelling in canine fashion 'Which way did it go?' I remember the story someone wrote about shooting in the wild cliff jungle that used to extend from Lyme Regis in the last century. You used to go out, one or two of you, with guns and there was no need to take dogs because after a minute or two had elapsed from the report of a gun the first of the Lyme Regis dogs would appear, eager to quest for you.

Partridge need a very steady dog – the sort that one means to have but never quite achieves. I think dogs take after their masters and on that basis there is little doubt that I am unsteady: I certainly enjoy seeing a good chase. I sometimes suggest the name of someone who wants to beat and thus exercise himself and his dog. 'Of course the dog will be on a lead,' I say, but my head keeper is quite adamant. 'You just can't afford to have them.' It is quite true that people whose dogs have to be on leads are often unable to hold them when the supreme moment comes and so often a partridge will get up when one is strung on a barbed wire fence. Hares are a great temptation and the line quavers as one picks up speed just ahead of us. Unfortunately there have not been enough hares on our Shoot in the last couple of years to give either experience or great cause for concern. It is not only the risk of dogs chasing that one has to consider but many people need to shout at or reprimand their dogs on such an occasion and that is something else that is not wanted. I am a little deaf myself, but conscious of my own stop and turn whistle sounding at intervals while I wonder what effect the cacophony of the innumerable 'silent' whistles has on the tensed partridge.

So on the whole partridge beaters are better off without dogs, but I speak for our Shoot only since on others it will depend on the amount of cover and hedge work involved: I doubt if anyone has as little as we have.

If the keeper has a reliable dog he may well prefer to handle any spot that needs a dog himself or have one reliable lieutenant to do the job. Beaters, however, have to get what satisfaction they can out of their heavy work and those of our beaters who have dogs would take themselves elsewhere if their dogs were not permitted on the Shoot. Not quite a question of 'Love me, love my dog,' because these are very good dogs. So we have quite a few dogs on the Shoot and with one exception all are springers: springers because our connected pheasant Shoots are for springers only. The little dogs that do all the hard work are not robbed of the pleasure of a retrieve by great big and not always amiable retrievers who would take all the credit for the birds they bring in with such grace and ease and yet not share the barbed wire work. I have no doubt that there is a place for the retriever in picking-up.

If you can afford it in terms of manpower I have no doubt that a picker-up is an asset. Where a drive may cover a very large area it is necessary to get the beaters back into the trailer and off to the next drive as soon as possible. The Guns are likely to have more time before moving off but it is a great strain on a Gun who has a bird down and who is casting further and wider while his fellow Guns are either on their way or waiting for him in a vehicle. On our hillside it is sometimes not necessary for the beaters to descend from the brow of the hill and so birds that are down must be left to such dogs as the Guns have brought or to a picker-up. In advocating a picker-up I cannot be compassionate towards those dogs belonging to the Guns, many of them chained to a peg while shooting takes place and rarely getting even a simple retrieve before being taken to the next peg: it is not in my interests to be so although a Gun's dog will always have precedence over mine should the Gun be using it to pick up. However it is a fact that one simple retrieve in a day brings enormous and obvious satisfaction to a dog and so such dogs may have their occasional retrieve and must then accept their proper station. Some Shoot captains are not at all keen on Guns bringing dogs with them. One Gun was telling me how upset his dog was to realise that morning that he was to be left behind. 'But,' he said, 'the last time I was here the Major said "I see some of you have brought your dogs with you: very well, that's all right as long as you keep them under control".' It was not a welcoming speech.

A picker-up may have very little work to do on a partridge Shoot but when the birds are shot off a hillside his observation of their flight from away behind the line can be rewarding. A pricked bird may collapse two hundred yards behind the line after the Gun has registered his shot as a miss. Not only that, the picker-up, although under the command and control of the captain of the Guns is in an advantageous position to mark where the coveys go and whence they came and must make a report on all these things to the keeper. After the Shoot is over he will further report on the general behaviour of the birds and perhaps have a suggestion to make which will lead to the improvement of the Shoot. I hope that no one will take me so literally as to make a suggestion to anyone at a Shoot, whatever that person's rank or position until the critic has been beating or shooting long enough to have become well accepted and until he knows that suggestions will be well received. As in many walks of life the rule for people joining a line of beaters is to say nothing for the first five years! Fortunately on our Shoot we enjoy a discussion over a pint of beer when the day has finished and everyone is welcome to contribute to this.

Either in deference to my age or to silence my dog whistle I am often selected as a picker-up. I certainly welcome this whether the plough be wet and sticky or the soil dry and sandy: one of the two always prevails! It also has the advantage that I can be recalled to the Colours when an extra hand is needed on a drive and when there is likely to be no urgent need of my services as a picker-up. My dog is no better than other dogs but performs the necessary duty well enough. It is, as I have said elsewhere, a great fillip for a dog to get a retrieve and I often think that if you have several dogs on a Shoot and wish to have a picker-up then, if there is no obvious candidate by reason of short legs or infirmity, it would be fair to let a different beater pick up after each drive.

The picker-up is the gentleman on the working side: I frequently get a brace of birds as a picker-up while the beaters do not. The Guns are grateful for one's presence and quick to praise the dog for confirming an uncertain shot. Their expressions of gratitude may be an indication of the value put upon a picker-up but are invidious to me: I know that I have the easy job and that my dog has all the interesting work. When I beat, my exhausting labour contributes but little to the general result, nevertheless I always feel then that any word of thanks extended to me has been fully merited.

I find that, just as with pheasants which have been shot, partridge have no hesitation in getting up and running and if you are not on the spot pretty quickly they will not be seen again. Someone has said that fifteen minutes is about the maximum time within which you can expect a dog to pick up a line. After that interval it is unlikely that he

A good retrieve. *Paul Middleton*

will find it. I am in no position to pontificate: I have had my successes and my failures. We have all had the Gun who says: 'There's a brace dead in those brambles and a winged bird just beyond!' and when the dog has been through the brambles twice one begins to feel the hopelessness of it. I have stood beside a Gun and said: 'That's dead', when a pheasant has folded up into a brake behind only to find it eventually a hundred yards beyond the point of fall. It is probably a good thing that there are so many beaters' shoots and certainly in our case that many of us shoot regularly. One cannot criticise anyone who says, 'A bird is down over there.' One has felt the same absolute certainly oneself, but whether you find a bird that is said to be down depends on more than your dog's nose.

I have found that the stone dead bird whether partridge or pheasant often presents a problem and the difficulty of finding a dead woodcock is commonly accepted. There was a pheasant shot on one of our shoots which fell in a sparse field of swedes. The Gun gave the distance and direction and, since we were about to beat that field and he was with us for that drive, showed a great and natural anxiety to take that place in the line. He was, however, sent to a more important hedge-line and a dog, good at retrieving, placed in that part of the line and its handler asked to look out for the bird. There were plenty of dogs but the bird was not found. At the end of that drive, since it was lunch-time, I offered to return with the Gun. We spent a lot of time with his dog, which is a flatcoat with a very good nose, and with mine but although we scanned the very open lines of swedes and the dogs quested with diligence we found no pheasant. It was as we gave up that I saw the very dead bird lying between the roots and perfectly visible although I must have looked past it a number of times and the dogs must have run nearby. Often as a picker-up I fail just as I fail when playing bridge to make a very careful initial appraisal and then act upon it. I was asked to go back for a Grey partridge, one of a right and left, which the Gun told me he had swung round to shoot at behind and at extreme range. He had been stationed at the end of the line. When I approached the scene two of the beaters with dogs were just questing at the other side of the field having covered the relevant part of one side, making their way towards a distant release pen which might have been a natural line for the bird to have taken. I started in the same way in the correct area and inevitably followed the footsteps of my colleagues who had by now gone on to take part in the next drive. Having drawn a complete blank though not under pressure to hasten my search as had been the case with my friends I returned to the start and mentally positioned the Gun in his proper place at the end of the line. I swung him round as he would have swung, according to his account, and started searching an area about fifty yards on. I had hardly reached the relevant area before the dog, questing across my front, picked up the bird. I paced it back to the position where I anticipated the Gun had stood and the distance was sixty paces. Of course the dog had covered that ground in his earlier and, to be fair, much wider sweeps. So if I were in a position to give advice, and of course I am not, I would suggest that all pickers-up should emulate the policeman who, whatever the cause of complaint or dispute, takes out his notebook and asks for a name and address and proceeds to take down the details. In other words one must first be sure of the Gun's position, of the swing, of the direction in which the bird was flying and the distance at which it was shot: I never am, of course. The Gun always shouts at me over his shoulder having tired of looking himself, having long left his original position and being concerned now only to get to his next peg!

KEEPERS AND BEATERS

> His brow was sad; his eye beneath
> Flashed like a falchion from its sheath,
> And like a silver clarion rung
> The accents of that unknown tongue,
>   'Excelsior!'
>   *Excelsior*,   H. W. Longfellow

When I was a small boy, and that is a long time ago, I often returned home carrying a rabbit after a day's exertion with a small friend, a couple of sticks and a field spaniel. My mother used to say: 'How useful that will be. We'll roast it on Thursday with the peas.' Possibly as the result of such constant encouragement I have always been phrenetic about rabbits. Now my head keeper uses the same tack to get his work done. He tells me about the big fox sitting eating a partridge outside the middle pen on the track – tame as any dog – does not want to leave, there every morning. He exaggerates the number of foxes I account for and thus I am pushed ever onwards getting up earlier each morning while my garden becomes overgrown and my letters remain unwritten. I do not know what my head keeper tells Taryn but the consequence is that he is happy to spend the whole Sunday with his terriers digging out a fox earth. It is the same story whether it be the small boy who wishes to become a gamekeeper who spends the whole of several days going around creosoting pens (I wonder if he has learnt vital lessons as to the drudgery of gamekeeping from this experience?) or the team of three or four men setting out to erect pens.

Ever since my retirement I have been the envy of every part time game preserver and sportsman. Alas I have never had so little time for shooting. Instead I have a regular vermin round in February and March or a little longer if I can be persuaded, and a like round for August and September with a general responsibility for vermin all the year. It is fair to say that the heavy burden of the four months' regular work is about to be lifted from me as we are fixing up a rota system this year taking it in turn each morning to get round the vermin line. In the meantime I fill

The long wait . . . *From a photograph by Paul Middleton*

in gaps and release partridge. All this is very necessary from the head keeper's point of view. He has a full time job elsewhere. He starts work early in the morning and thus has a little free time in the afternoons as the days lengthen. To keep himself fully occupied he keepers a sizeable pheasant Shoot as well as looking after the partridge Shoot. You can see that its a full time job and why he has to count on service and obedience from us all.

We? We are the second syndicate of whom I speak elsewhere. They have the kindness to make me an honorary member in return for my odd job convenience. It is a sad fact that I am not thrilled at the thought of shooting the birds I have cherished. I am not enamoured of the very long wait that most partridge drives require offering in return little of the varied interests that a wait outside a good pheasant covert will provide. No doubt I am influenced by the fact that at the end of my wait I am likely to see several high birds go over with a complete disregard for my shot and go on to risk the love and affection I have lavished upon them by sailing over my neighbour's gun.

The beaters are enjoined to masochism even as I am. They are young. They are fit. They are keen. On any three days beating on our ground you can reckon on one being wet. When it's wet you sink deeply into the light chalk. When this light soil is wet it is remarkably sticky. When you walk the dry plough you sink as deeply. Someone with a pedometer notched up ten and a half miles one day, all up and down impossible hillsides of course. Each beater is, or by chance has become, a sportsman. All shoot and gradually more and more have dogs, very good ones too, but above all they are good partridge beaters. They are perhaps ingenuous since the profits are scarcely worth the effort but they are in the way of being idealists since they also beat on a nearby pheasant Shoot in return for a beater's shoot and a few roost shoots. Yet that is the only Shoot I know where fifteen or sixteen beaters are always present: who beat well and are subject to discipline. On some of the other Shoots where I have the privilege of beating, countrymen, farm workers and the like chat noisily (but always with wit) when being conveyed and in the course of their beating. They know their way about and do a good job but they don't run and don't look to be told how to do their work. The partridge beater on a downland Shoot is a different kettle of fish. Round goes the signal to the left flanker to get round the covey. Run must the hedgerow beater who has just seen a covey making off across Thirty Two acres.

At the start of a drive my head keeper always imposes a sensible delay. Not to get the Guns in position for there will normally have been time

Fit, keen beaters. *Paul Middleton*

enough for that but to get every man properly spaced out over the very wide front that we cover. Then, when things have long appeared to us to be perfect enough and the flankers, armed with their flags, are waiting well ahead at each end of the line we get the hand signal to start or, if we are on an irregular line maybe, one side only will be waved forward. Just before the pen in the centre fence running along our axis the line will stop while the bit of rough ground around the pen is searched out. One does not see everything that goes on though much of the line is visible and various signs are passed on. A hand pointing to the left and you may see a few shapes running ahead there. You point also and the keeper picking up the signal slows down the other side of the line. The birds are away to the left and the left flanker is waving his flag before they have left the ground. Once they are airborne and have assumed their direction it is almost impossible to turn them and when they seem determined on a course of safety, shouts and waving from the beaters to try to deflect them are not out of order. Indeed one must jump and wave one's arms but despite that they generally carry on to be safe for another day or perhaps for another drive because someone, probably a flanker, will have watched their descent. At the cross hedges the whole line will stop some fifty yards back having been brought parallel to it while the keeper and his safe dog walk along it from one end and a reliable dog does the same from the other end. Birds will be pegged here for there is a little close cover but it is only the occasional bird that

Once more unto the entanglements. *Paul Middleton*

suffers, to the chagrin of its handler. Onwards goes the line towards the crest of the hill and the axis of our advance is the strip of plough that has been run up the centre so that the birds too may have a highway in the right direction. Now the odd bird, preceded by the shrill warning of the keeper's whistle, takes to the air and the sound of the guns betokens the success of the drive. Sometimes several shots, two doubles and a single, tell where a bird has swung high round the contour, offering a shot to several. It is not until one has stood in a line of Guns, waiting before a vast empty skyline, that one learns to appreciate the enormous importance of that warning whistle. Whenever the birds come they have the gift of coming unexpectedly it seems, but when they appear silently and unheralded over that empty nothingness they seem to be over and away long before one has time to assess their line and to pick one's bird.

As the last of the beaters clears his area of cover by the wall all are able to look down upon the Guns. The final whistle goes: it is pleasant then for the beaters to see every gun being returned to its slip as they cross the wall. The nature of partridge shooting in the downs is such that beaters are frequently exposed to the Guns as they come over the brow towards which the Guns are shooting. The distances are, however, reasonable and we have never had any trouble or experienced a feeling of danger. On some grounds and one in particular where I beat a sloping area of kale, one hears an extraordinary screech from the guns as they are fired although these are directed at high birds and well away from the beaters. There is no danger but something in the nature of the fall of the land there seems to produce that ominous sound.

I am a keen advocate of the use of a horn to start and finish a drive: it is a sound that is clear, decisive and audible to all. Not only as a matter of safety but as a clear warning to the furthermost Guns. One such was very aggrieved recently as he panted up long after the Guns were in position for the drive, having been unaware that the previous drive had finished. As a picker-up I find it useful when I have stayed behind looking for a bird to know that the next beat has started and to gauge my movements accordingly. A horn would not be much good at the distant start of some of our drives perhaps and the feeling seems to be against using one on our Shoot so mine is a lone voice.

Beaters get a keen vicarious pleasure from their work. Although they may themselves be mediocre shots it is important to them that a fair toll is taken of the birds they put up. The single shot as a bird goes forward out of sight is reward enough. The good and sportsmanlike Shot is always noted and the Gun who can let the low birds pass and bring down the high ones is the object of admiration. There is indeed little in it for the beaters. They may get a ten pound note at the end of the day but that is not an economic reward. Every so often a dog will suffer a gash from barbed wire which will necessitate two or three visits to the vet and account for whatever has been earned in the year. Leggings and waterproof trousers have a short life and thorn proof coats are no match for barbed wire particularly at the end of a long wet day. Probably as important as the pay are the facilities afforded to beaters. Sometimes there is a convenient shed where lunch may be taken in comfort on straw bales. Sometimes beaters are expected to find their own accommodation round the farm buildings or in their cars. Personally I would most value the Shoot as it affected my dog: the prospect of suitable cover, sufficient birds and one or two decent retrieves. A nip of whisky at lunchtime adds warmth to my day. In my experience, the rougher the Shoot the better the treatment and courtesy extended to the beaters. I well remember overhearing the captain of the Guns on a small Shoot addressing them as I wandered nearby at the start of the day: 'Remember also each one of you to make a point of thanking the beaters at the end of the day.' I do not suppose it would be thought necessary or politic to say such a thing to the Guns on the majority of Shoots – but it is! On the rougher Shoots, if I may take the liberty of so describing them, I find the Guns much more ready to suggest that a beater leaves his birds with them while he goes on to the next drive. It is in these little things that the beater finds comfort.

Having said so much about the beaters one must go on to say that they are, like the partridge itself, a source of some wonder; not of course as to their life style but as to their willingness, indeed keenness, to beat in the first place. On a downland partridge Shoot I think they do the hardest work they could find.

TIMING

> 'Where are they?' said Mr Winkle, in a state of highest excitement turning round and round in all directions, 'Where are they? Tell me when to fire, where are they – where are they?'
> ...
> 'We shall very likely come up with another covey in five minutes', said the long gamekeeper, 'if the gentleman begins to fire now, perhaps he'll just get the shot out of the barrel by the time they rise.'
>
> *Pickwick Papers,* Dickens

THE JANUARY RELEASE

When should the birds go down? If you are a purist then I suppose they should go down in late January. This will give them time to learn about their new habitat, seek a mate and raise a family. Did you say you were a purist? One learns from Mr Allington's essay, published by Kynoch Ltd in *Shooting Notes and Comments* (1910), that:

> Hungarians will stay best if they have been bought in January and turned out on ground which has been heavily shot. When let out in February, on or about the middle of the pairing season, their thoughts are turned more towards love-making than to exploring fresh country, and it will be found that the higher price charged for the birds at this time of year will be more than counter-balanced by the number which remain to nest.

I do not know what a 'Hungarian' is but I do know that releasing a few hundred birds in January or February is not likely to be very successful on a small unkeepered Shoot of the sort we run. So we do not attempt to do it that way.

It is easier to release much closer to the first shoot day and I know of three ways in which this can be done.

AN AMERICAN WAY

The first is much frowned upon and I do not advocate it. Were it to be practised in this country it might well be prohibited before long by Act of Parliament as was the shooting of pigeon from traps years ago. It is described by Dr Jean Delacour in her book, *Pheasant Breeding and Care*. In a chapter devoted to the pheasant on shooting preserves, she recommends an area of three to four hundred acres as the basis for the Shoot and blocks of thirty to forty acres for each four man Shoot. Buffer zones between the various blocks provide for safety. Dr Delacour says that a 70 per cent recovery rate may be anticipated and recommends releasing the birds some thirty to sixty minutes ahead of the sportsmen's arrival for the best recovery rate!

Recovery rates fascinate me: I am always looking for the flaw in the claim. But quite genuine claims can be made in respect of many of the 'put and take' pheasant Shoots in this country. If partridge are successfully released on such a pheasant Shoot and persuaded to stay, then by virtue of taking a few at each of the succeeding pheasant days I think the partridge put down may well be annihilated. Dr Delacour might feel at home on some of these Shoots as they swell their recovery rate by beating the home pen for the second time!

The suggestion that some Shoots in this country have indulged in the type of release advocated by Dr Delacour has caused the sporting press to throw its hands up in horror. An understandable aversion to the thought of throwing up a bird to be shot at, has been expressed, coupled with indignation at the excessive number of birds said to be put over the Guns on some Shoots. The two are not necessarily connected, of course. It is interesting that in this day of the common man, it should be the common vulgarity of the latter practice in particular, which raises the ire of the dignified leader writers of the sporting press. Could their ancestors, I wonder, be among those who went all the way to Monte Carlo to shoot pigeon from traps and for whom the special pigeon guns in use today were made? Were they the same people who tempted royalty with the massed *battue*?

Me? I do not think much of it, either. I am just a mischief maker and speaking as a member of the beating line feel I am entitled to be cynical!

At any rate, partridge lend themselves very readily to malpractices of that sort. The suspicion is that Shoots rear birds for next to nothing or buy in young poults and then throw these over the hedge to unsuspecting shooters at anything from £13 to £30 a time. These birds fly, as we

A high shot. *From a photograph by Paul Middleton*

all know they can fly, from the moment they obtain their freedom. The Guns are pleased with their sport and only too happy to pay for their birds and for those picked up in the roots in the afternoon – 'Must've been pricked in the first drive, Sir.' Well – the total picked up at that drive was certainly less than might have been expected from the great number of shots fired!

Whatever the suspicion about some Shoots, it must be said that many of those offering shooting by the day or by the bird enjoy the highest reputation.

Partridge shooting as a sport will die when the emphasis ceases to be on birds which have been brought through the winter, on wild birds and on birds properly released, full of life and vigour; a number of which will remain after release in an environment attractive to them. It would be easy to release a thousand birds in lots of two or three hundred and walk away after the final shoot: it would save a great deal of time and trouble. From that one could progress to putting birds down a shorter and shorter time before each shoot and using younger and younger birds. The costs of the Shoot would get less and less: just a supply of pellets and a little wheat.

I do not know how you could stop that: how can the shooter tell? Red-legs could certainly be released in bulk and driven from some sort of jumping off point in reasonably small numbers. It is very difficult. If the dogs peg more than the Guns shoot, that is a suspicious circumstance. In such circumstances the Gun is unlikely to be told how many birds have been pegged though he may be charged for them. Again, many an innocent act is committed in circumstances of darkest suspicion and the pegging may be due to other factors. Of course this only applies to Red-legs: Greys do not like being pegged! Red-legs should have plenty of colour about them at twelve weeks of age and one would not expect to be shooting them before that. I suppose the same applies to the Ogridge – but what is an Ogridge? No doubt a first cross comes out with certain standard characteristics but we had some with slaty legs which appeared to be fit and strong but although we had them with us until all characteristics of the juvenile should have left them, they persisted in their slaty legs. So there seems to be no guide for the sportsman. He must look to it for himself remembering that if one ceases to put as much into the sport as one gets out of it, it is no longer sport.

So the bodies that govern our sport are in the process of making a rule, or issuing advice, to the effect that no birds should be released after the first shots have been fired on any particular Shoot. The Game

Conservancy do not commit themselves to any public condemnation of the sort of practices I have described although they no doubt feel as strongly as anyone about the matter. Their justification for the new rule is that by over shooting, particularly where relays of birds are released, the ground is scoured and the natural wild stock are bound to be swept away, a few at a time perhaps, but inevitably, with the relays of freshly released birds. Although one cannot point to the magpie as an example of the wild being annihilated and although it may be the case that some of the estates whose wild life, it is suggested, would be so abused, had no game on them in the first place; the logic is there and it is right that the sport should regulate its own affairs in this manner.

TOPPING UP

So while we may not be able to afford the approach to release advocated by Mr Allington and are not allowed to release in the manner advised by Dr Delacour, we are incidentally prohibited from releasing in a manner which has been successfully practised on our Shoot and, indeed, on many others, for some time. I need not go into the finer points of 'topping up' or 'staggered release' because it is no longer a permitted variation. It was a method which gave satisfactory results where satisfactory results are exceeding hard to come by. No doubt much of the fascination of dealing with partridge is that the released bird is always wild: you do not see long lines of them snaking after the keeper. To the partridge man there is no comparision to be made between that bird and the pheasant. You release your stock of pheasant in a wood and there the livelier ones spend about six weeks finding out about the woods and cover about them: others hang around the pen until the last shoot. On the last day you ask the keeper how many birds are left and he will tell you that there are about fifty in the pen, twenty in Hither Wood, five hens and a cock in Yonder Wood, and the old white cock still in the farmyard. Indeed they will still be there when the Guns assemble. You can ask your keeper about the partridge and he will tell you that there is a covey of wild Greys in the roots and several coveys of Red-legs in such and such a stubble field, but on the day some will be drifting over the boundary as the Guns assemble. Some will fly as the beaters enter the first field and others will simply have disappeared.

Having found a satisfactory way of releasing and holding the birds it will be hard for many of us to start again.

OUR OWN PROPOSALS

The third method of release which I go on to describe is that which we shall try. It may not be the best method but in the partridge world where there are many amateur keepers, many part timers and very few full time keepers (I exclude keepers who have charge of both pheasant and partridge) there seem to be few channels of communication and very little information on release procedures is passed around. It may be appropriate, therefore, if with suitable caution, I set out the principles which will govern our releases in future.

Now the first thing a person hoping to release partridge looks for is habitat and having found what he thinks is the right land and land which is sympathetically farmed, he makes a New Year's resolution about predators. He does these things because the Game Conservancey, quite rightly, tell him to. What terrible disappointment follows! On two of the pheasant Shoots where I beat, an experiment was conducted and fifty partridge were released with the pheasant. The two Shoots are not connected in any way nor, as far as I can recall, were the releases made in the same year. Both Shoots seemed to have excellent land: plenty of rough, plenty of wood, thick hedges and reasonable cultivation. In neither case were the birds seen once they had left the pens, although in one case a number remained in the pens for quite some time. In another case I seized the opportunity to beat at the second meeting of a new partridge Shoot. I think they had only put two hundred birds down, proposing to increase the number the following season. It was in a very nice valley with several ins and outs but surrounded by large, and I fear from our point of view, sterile fields. We shot one bird that day and I did in fact, see six! I have a host of stories of a like nature. So, habitat and predation; yes, but what do they mean and what else?

In a splendid article written in *The Pageant of Nature vol.2 British Wild life and its Wonders* published in 1923, Frank Bonnett refers to the adaptability of the partridge to the circumstances of civilisation; its adaptability, that is, compared with other birds. 'The more surprising,' he says, 'seeing that he has to put up with no small share of persecution during the shooting season.' His habits, Mr Bonnett says, have adapted readily enough to altered conditions, 'so that instead of retiring to the wilder and uncultivated parts of the country, the bird actually prefers to have its being in the midst of man's activities whenever he finds he can exploit them to his own advantage. The partridge, in fact, always has a preference for cultivated districts, for there, by the constant turning of the soil he is enabled to thrive the better.'

So rough herbage, weed and hedgerow may not of itself suffice although it will be a helpful start. Probably the greatest help for the partridge has been the promotion by the Game Conservancy of a policy of unsprayed headlands and that is probably the first step to be taken towards creating a suitable habitat. Cultivation, you see, also forms part of the desirable habitat.

Habitat is only the first step, even then, although you must bear in mind that I am concerned with areas which no longer support a modest but natural, wild stock. Having found or provided the right habitat, we think, from our experience, that it is important that a partridge be released, all unaware, as it were,

1. Into a world where it recognises convenient sources of the food to which it is accustomed and the places where it is set out.
2. Into a world where it is held by the calls and companionship of its fellows.

To achieve these things, and I suppose the last in particular, a carefully programmed release is essential. It is a matter of timing: your timing must start with the receipt of the birds and shooting dates must follow from that. Unless you are in a very fortunate position the birds cannot come until harvest is over or they will lose themselves in the standing crops. Nor, if you are in a position to get the birds before harvest, should you think you can necesarily advance your shooting dates. You will phase your release over a longer period.

So, let us say that 1 September is your start date and that you have a kind landlord who is not going to burn the stubbles throughout that month. Now the next point is: how are you going to arrange the distribution of your birds? If you have ten release pens you can fix six hundred birds in three deliveries of twenty to a pen. You could and may be forced to increase the population of each pen to thirty and in that case you will only have two deliveries. The same formula will take care of a thousand birds in twenty pens but with as many pens and fewer birds, we do not think you want to reduce the deliveries below two. Where you are short of space you will be able to take advantage of the double pen system by putting a greater number in the pens and opening the pophole between the sections. When you are ready to start releasing, the birds awaiting release can be confined to one section while they wait their turn. As I have already said, I can no longer base my advice on established practice. Our own view, nevertheless, is that a gradual build-up of birds is the best because they will hold better thus treated. Therefore we would opt for twenty to a pen if we were able to effect a satisfactory release in terms of time. Generally, with the first shoot looming, time will be lacking.

Your schedule might run something like this for a six hundred bird release:

Week 1	First shoot day minus 7 weeks
	300 birds to pen (30 to each pen)
	Minus 6 weeks and 3 days
	Release 5 birds from each pen
Week 2	Minus 6 weeks
	Release 10 birds from each pen
	Minus 5 weeks and 3 days
	Release remaining 15 birds from each pen
	(N.B. If you are unable to obtain the second delivery on this day, then only 10 or 12 birds should be released. The other 3 or 4 birds remain as callers until the second delivery arrives)
	Minus 5 weeks and 3 days
	Top up, 300 birds at 30 to each pen
Week 3	Minus 4 weeks and 6 days
	Release 10 birds from each pen
	Minus 4 weeks and 3 days
	Release 10 birds from ech pen
Week 4	Minus 4 weeks
	Release 5 birds from each pen
Week 5	Minus 3 weeks
	Release the 5 remaining birds (the callers) unless they are to be kept as suggested below
First shoot day	Close the popholes of release sections and where callers have been retained remove any which may be upset by the shooting

Thus at the beginning of the fourth week you will have released all your birds in a three week programme and you will still have four weeks before the first shoot. This is one week more than the minimum of three weeks which is thought to be fair and sporting. This extra week is your emergency time: a very short time it is too. If there has been a burst of interference by predators, weather or cultivation (and something always does happen) then you may be forced to delay one of your releases in order to treat your outbreaks of gapes or merely to retain the holding and calling power of a number of penned birds where others outside have been seriously disturbed. If this occurs in the course of releasing the first delivery then you will have to get the second delivery postponed for a week. Let us hope that you have already arranged for this possibility. In the case of the second delivery you have more freedom for not only have you the extra week but if necessary the first shoot can be postponed.

Fortunately the double pen release system gives you an insurance against bad weather since the birds are released quite easily into the second pen where they find the same protection as that which they have left.

I should say, that if we had more time, we would certainly keep the first birds in the pens for a full week before starting the release. It may also be worth mentioning, that having achieved a reasonable release of the first lot it is possible to speed the release of subsequent deliveries.

Now the callers remain in the pens to be released three weeks before the first shoot, but there is another way of dealing with them. The callers may be left in the pens throughout the season. On shooting days any that are likely to be disturbed by the shooting will be removed to safer quarters in the early morning (you will have some spare release sections). At the end of the season these callers, who will number no less than fifty, if you leave five in each of the ten pens, can be kept as breeding stock. If you are thinking of breeding, then here you will have birds already caught up, untouched by shot and, I would think, very suitable for egg production. If you are not breeding your own birds then these callers can be released as super, fit healthy breeding stock at just about the time that Mr Allington thought appropriate.

VERMIN

> Where ignorance is bliss,
> 'Tis folly to be wise.
>
> *Ode on a Distant Prospect of Eton College,*   Thomas Gray

Standing on the overgrown track beside the barley now just turning one sees nothing. On the other side the wide verge which we manured in the spring is chest high with nettles, dock and other weeds. Somewhere at the same height is the newly laid hedge, thick and growing well but at the moment a host to every weed that grows. On the far side the corn merges with the hedge: there is a deep sea of green and if you venture into it without parting the nettles you are sure to fall. There is life on the weeds, caterpillars and greenfly, but what else is there here? The birds and their July broods are somewhere out in the corn in their own world: an island community, or perhaps tracing a circuit designed to keep them out of the way of vermin. Perhaps there is a bare patch somewhere, if so it will be well used: I have no idea. To the unknowing eye at any rate there is no sign of a run through the weeds. No fox run, no run of lesser vermin, no parting of the grass where a partridge enters the thick. At such times one may feel that nothing can be done to protect the birds, there is no sign of battle or pursuit. They have been here, there are droppings further down the track: all is well. No doubt on a keepered Shoot nests would have been marked and a much more thorough survey made of areas of predation or its risk.

Nothing can be done now and nothing much can alter the fact that so many hundred birds will be released here in September and save for some out of the ordinary occurrence nothing much is going to prevent the usual numbers going over the Guns. If vermin are at work the lack of the odd wild covey or two will not be noticed by many of the Guns nor will it make any difference to numbers in the bag. Yes it is easy to be complacent when reared birds are released. In such circumstances one works very hard to keep down vermin for very little profit. Better by far to lower the hatching percentage or put in a few extra eggs and have a few extra birds on the estate that no one knows about. When you are congratulated you shake your head and speak about the work that has been put in on the vermin.

It is no good keeping the traps going all the year round if there are rats at the pens or at the release sites. For one thing if the traps have been set properly they will be catching an undue number of rats which is probably an uneconomic way to use such traps; certainly on an unkeepered Shoot. Rats are likely to attract and offer the hospitality of their warrens to those vermin who prey on rats and where the one multiplies so will the other. So the rats must be cleared off first and I will deal with rats and with foxes elsewhere in this book.

Our vermin work is open to criticism and we are aware of that. To be effective a vermin round on an unkeepered estate has to be well organised and the organiser will often feel that it would be quicker to do the job himself – only he has no time. From time to time a person will be found who will devote a regular time each day to this service but such persons tend to come and go and even they may balk at a seven day week! It is possible to use the traps at the same time as snaring is in progress: that way whoever is on the fox round can look at the traps. Or perhaps, as in one case I know, there is an open track running the length of the Shoot and a quick journey along that by car will give adequate supervision to a restricted line of traps without interfering with the driver's normal work. The trapping of small vermin is well documented and some good tips are to be found in the books. There is no need for me to go into the technicalities, whether they concern mammals or birds, but make no mistake about it, the work is important.

My head keeper seldom sets a trap in what you would call a natural site. One reason is that there is a scarcity of such sites and when you take into account the need for protection against other livestock and the need on a Shoot such as ours to be able to pin-point such traps without difficulty when called upon to take over a round you can see why he prefers the ambuscade. This, after a great deal of digging and piling up of earth, looks like a miniature railway junction. We throw up lots of little banks and deep ways and anything that gets into the maze generally ends up at the mouth of a six inch pitch-fibre pipe of which we have a small supply. They are just large enough to allow a trap to be sprung and there is generally a trap at each end. Once the grass has grown there is no longer any sign of these earthworks but the knowledgeable, peering through the parted nettles, can make out the outline of a hole, protected from the inquisitive bird by a couple of sticks across its mouth. Some people think that a little weed killer round the approach will make investigation by a weasel more likely. Whether the patch is bare or overgrown one should beware of adders, making a sufficient disturbance for them to move away. Your dog, sitting patiently behind you, will lean forward stretching out his nose to get himself bitten by an adder if you give him half a chance.

Magpies do not seem to suffer much on the roads: an occasional crow on early morning patrol for road victims will suffer the fate of those he is seeking but I do not see many magpies. Dave had a right and left at magpie from our little pheasant wood last season but I am always surprised on the Shoots I visit at the absence of magpies when the beaters step into the wood. The magpie is extremely wary and has few enemies, effective enemies at any rate. I think the numbers we get rid of do no more than ease the lot of those that remain! Crows too multiply and our efforts against them are not significant.

I went to quite a lot of trouble over a crow in a large ash tree this year. I sat all evening under a hedge tunnel ready to creep forward when the cock landed for the night so that I might make a good job of it. Alas! His raucous cry sounded from behind and above as he flew over but it was apparent that I had been detected. Within .22 range of the nest was an old shed with a boarded window facing the right direction. I tracked down the farmer and obtained authority to force open the window. All evening till past dark I sat there, shuffling and smoking. I could have better spent the time down the hill at another nest: nothing came. The next day happening to meet young Mark, he said: 'No wonder, I shot her yesterday as she rose from the nest.' Two days later the dark line of the male, as I supposed it to be, showed above the nest as I viewed it from the hill above. Later that day I shot him from the hillside with a .22. This does emphasise the need to kill both birds if you are seeking effective control. I had much the same experience with a magpie a day or two later but this time I was not so successful.

One does find that the breeding season for feathered vermin is a very short one and it comes when gardening is at its peak. It is not so much a question of spending an hour here or there but of the need to explore many miles of hedgerow and the need to deal with every nest found at very much the same time. I am sure that on our own Shoot the solution is to give every member of the second syndicate a small area for which he is to be responsible. He can have the interest of bringing to book a pair of magpies or crows which will represent a few pleasant evening walks with the dog and a few evenings of ambush and it will be something that he can do thoroughly and for the good of all. Perhaps there should be a forfeit for those found later with a nest still on their patch!

If there is a keen man in the syndicate with sufficient time, perhaps an air rifle specialist, he can be very helpful with magpie problems. My head keeper tells of a method he used with success, simpler than staking out a dead rabbit or sheep's eyes in fur and that was to put a rabbit on the track near a likely place of concealment and run a car over it. One morning at first light he had done this and was lying absolutely concealed in the scrub when he heard the shuffle, shuffle, tap, tap of the tramp who regularly made his way down to the village by that route. With a prepared line of sight through the undergrowth to the remains on the road and his gun ready my head keeper heard the wayfarer pause. For a second a hand was poised above the gory remains then, shuffle, shuffle, tap, tap – the bait had been taken!

It is a sad reflection on the state of our Shoot, though it must be common to many, that I think the time has come when we can afford to have a spring magpie drive! The built up areas around our Shoot provide undisturbed nesting areas and superb foraging for magpies and there is little that we can do about that. Towards the end of May when gauche young birds abound these tend to explore further afield to the open downs and the sheep pens. What my head keeper has in mind is a foray by all the members of the second syndicate. This may well start at dawn with the members of the syndicate slipping in at the extremities of the Shoot, skirting the hedgerows with frequent pauses. One would expect a few magpies to glide down ahead, out of range no doubt, and these should be met by one or other of the Guns coming from the opposite direction. Within a couple of hours members of the syndicate would be meeting at the centre of the Shoot. Who knows what luck we may have? No doubt any vacancies thus created in magpie territory will be quickly filled but we shall have done something positive.

RATS, RATS AND RATS

> He hath made everything beautiful in his time: also he hath set the world in their heart, so that no man can find out the work that God maketh from the beginning to the end.
>
> Ecclesiastes IV. 11

I wonder what that means? I like to think that it means that it is not for us to hope to understand the purpose of such an animal as the rat who can live in the midden yet emerge clean, live healthily and well in the midst of filth and decay and whose name is synonymous with disease and corruption. A rat is indeed a thing of beauty; one just wonders?

'Rats are not a problem.' That at any rate is what my farmer friend said to me when I pointed to my terrier digging at the bottom of Caius wood. 'It is just a matter of systematic poisoning.' To do him justice his farm does not have a rat problem: so it upsets me to see rat holes around the partridge pens on our bordering Shoot. Every year the rats were ferreted – adding to the available sport and I suppose that with the end of serious feeding in December the rats moved on to their normal winter haunts. They do seem able to live anywhere and upon anything. Apart from their habit of eating the floorboards and the insulation once they get into a house, from which they may not derive any great nourishment, they do very well on sewerage and more important they seem to thrive near farm slurry ditches and that means certain survival during the hardest part of the year. I say this because I have a baiting point half way down a slurry ditch while away in the distance other baiting points control entrance to and egress from this particular site – I am talking of distances of two or three hundred yards. The bait at this particular point has been regularly taken since it was placed there over a period of about four weeks. To my annoyance a beater, walking the adjoining swedes, told me that he had had to pursue and kill a baby rat there the other day, so the battle is still on. Of course in this land of open country there are vast grain fields that offer food and cover throughout the growing season and food from the moment the fresh grain is sown until the

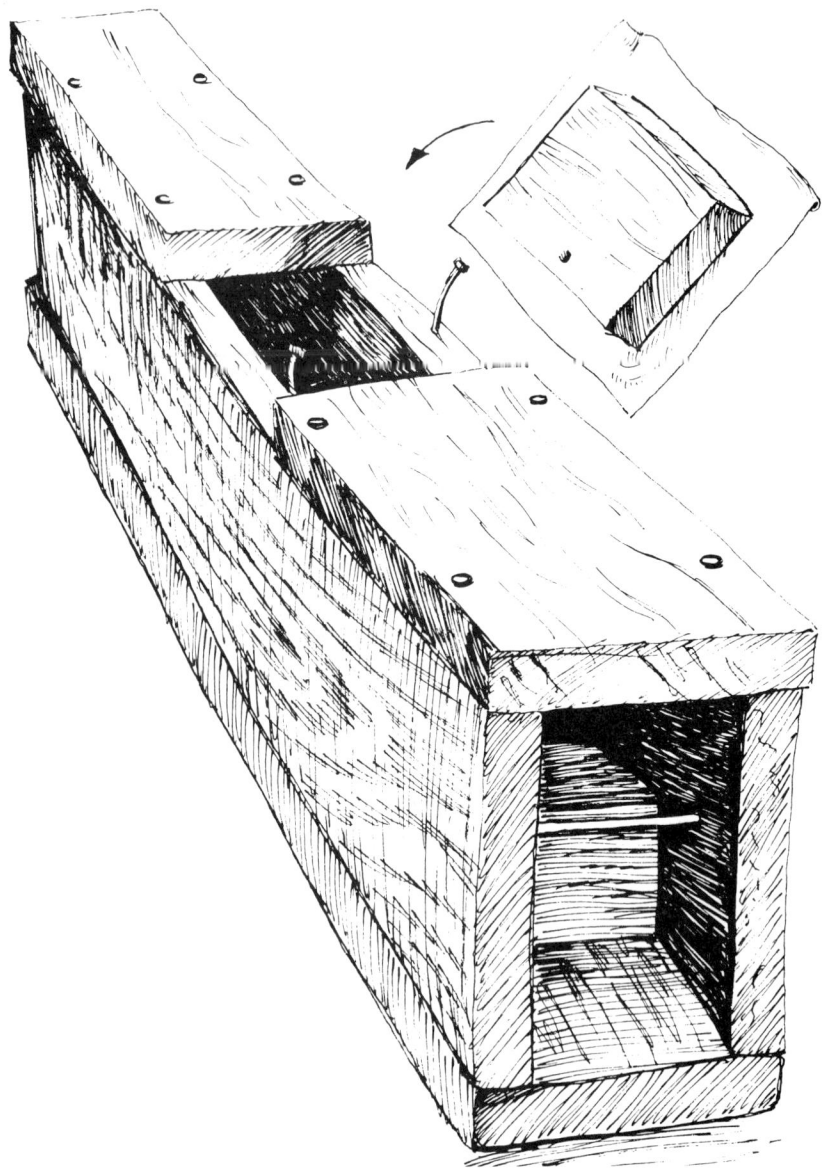

The tunnel rat baiter

plough once more turns the soil. The problem is that thousands of happy families are evicted from the corn during harvest and find their way to the sheltered hedgerows and banks where they may pass the winter. From there they make their way, it seems, hither and thither seeking old or new haunts or perhaps just expanding.

At any rate, I said to my head keeper this year: 'Rats are no problem, it is merely a question of systematic poisoning.' I went on to say that no Shoot should allow rats – not on any part of a Shoot. Furthermore I said that I would deal with the rat problem. Was I not after all the vermin man? At this stage the harvest was in full swing and one could at last get near the pens. These were in some cases being erected and volunteers could be found on any weekend levelling off the ground, creosoting, fitting top nets or delivering water. The land seemed virgin and untenanted although I noticed a large rat near one pen which had obviously suffered death during harvest operations.

So I began and like all foolish amateurs was to find that I had left all my preparations till too late. I had underestimated the problem and not fully understood the way to go about things.

I started by making rectangular box baiting points. Each had a lid in the middle held on by its fit and by a sawn off nail run through a hole at the edge of the lid into the side of the box. I found that a square of fertiliser bag nailed over the lid gave a watertight compartment. Within the box and beneath the lid nestled two plastic bags containing bait, held in place or rather prevented from being dragged out, by a couple of nails on each side. The box was about 4 in x 4 in x 2 ft 6 in. I found later that I had to modify the box by fixing a chuck or step of wood just inside each end to prevent grain being scratched out. Subject to that my boxes are satisfactory providing a safe dark feeding place for rats, unassailable by birds or the larger mammals and easy to check and replenish. They can be buried in the ground or placed under a shelter and are vastly more tidy than bits of slate, corrugated iron etc. Such a box is shown on page 108.

Having been promised a supply of old wood I waited a while before making the first half dozen and eventually had to put these few out at the pens as my further supplies did not materialise. It had been my innocent but misguided intention to place a baiting box on each side of each pen to distract and occupy the investigating swarms. When I placed out those that were available the first feeders had alrady been put out in readiness for the birds. The air was heavy with the odour of high protein pellets while grain was spread around the base of each feeding drum. Almost at once rats appeared – not many, just the odd one here

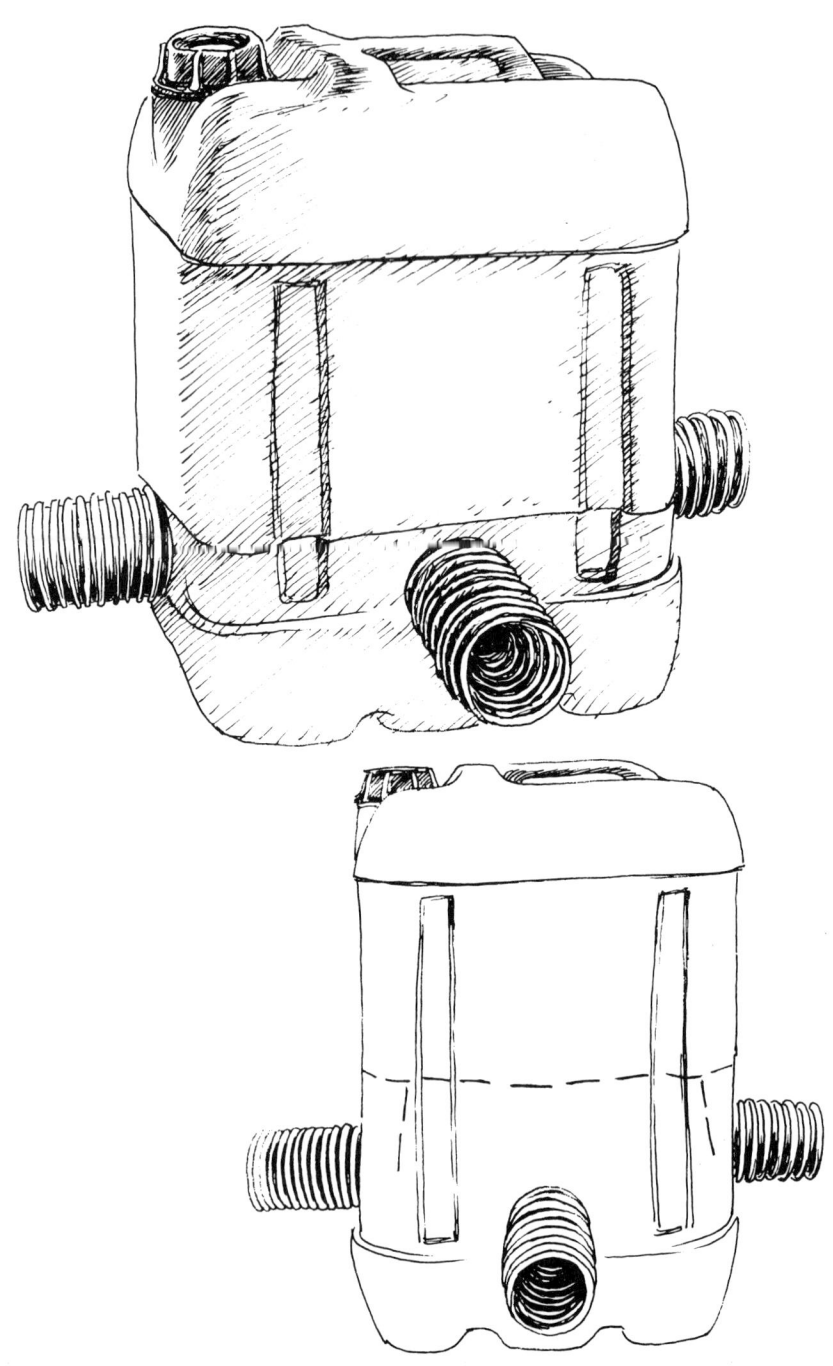

The plastic drum rat baiter

and there to indicate that there were many more behind. At the same time sudden little onslaughts on the bait showed that some rats were taking. About this time I learned about the plastic drum baiting system and prepared about twenty of those baiters.

Each plastic baiter is made by sawing a plastic drum or preferably a square type plastic container in half. In the lower half four vertical slits persuade it to allow the top half to fit down over it. In the bottom half three holes allow three four-inch sections of plastic land drain to be inserted as on page 114. In the bottom of the drum is placed a stone or broken ploughshare, it is surprising how many of these you will find if you have a purpose for them and these keep the drum stable and proof against wind. It is also necessary to bore two or more holes in the bottom of each drum to let any moisture out. As with the box baiter two bags of bait are placed inside, one split open. When a start is made on the second it is time to add another. It takes a few days for the rats to start taking. One can unscrew the cap of the drum to view the contents and pull the top half off to refill. I prefer to tie a piece of baling twine round my baiters so that the badgers cannot pull them apart.

I had great difficulty boring holes for the land drainage pipes at first but found that you can buy sets of round saws for hole cutting which fit an electric drill and one of these was the exact size to allow a section of drain pipe to be inserted and firmly held.

It was now November and with horror I realised that in addition to the holes around each pen there were small warrens along the hedge banks. Although the rats were seen less by day there were apparent signs of their activity. We had passed through a period of extremely wet and stormy weather and had lost birds from that cause. Now as November wore on some birds were attacked in the pens. A sage had warned me on seeing our rat problem, 'For goodness sake keep ample food in the pens because if the rats get short of food they will go for the birds.' And that is what they did despite ample food.

Bearing in mind the warnings against contaminating hands with poison or placing bait where the birds might find it I had cautiously kept it strictly to my baiters. Realising that with the massive amount of fresh damp grain and pellets available I was in danger of losing the battle I now started the second phase of my war and for this I procured a long narrow trowel. I then filled every hole that I could find with poisoned grain. I used great quantities of bait and used a spade to see that every hole was filled in. Closing holes in this manner observes the law relating to the placing of poisoned bait: it also ensures that every hole is dealt with. The next day you will always see one or two that you have missed and more importantly, if the hole remains closed, you can assume that the occupants are dead. In this way I seemed to be getting on top of the problem. Then one morning I would go and see at one pen a vast amount of digging while perhaps at another three or more holes would have been opened from the outside. Holes leading into the pens reappeared. Outside one pen birds were apparently attacked by rats while jugging. I had by now lost all caution in handling a very dangerous substance. I remember one morning using a small plastic sack in which several kilos of bait had been mixed. After an hour or so I noticed that my working hand was blue to the wrist. I obtained water and washed all the poison off: by the end of the morning my hands were blue again. I waited two days after that to die and detecting no signs of poisoning in myself was uncertain whether to rejoice or despair. Well, those of you who are as uninformed as I was should learn enough from this chapter to be able to conduct all your operations with far less effort and the assistance of rubber gloves.

It was now when the season was well advanced that I learnt that my baiting points should have been far from the pens, providing a distant and attractive ambush for the wandering rats: this is not easy. Although at any pen one can envisage two or perhaps three lines of hedgerow approach, when it comes to the point, one always seems to find oneself in the same position as when one first thinks of driving pheasants back along the hedges to their home cover in the evening, faced with an exhausting array of alternatives.

Each fixed point now had a radius of baiters (barrier baiting) and the holes at the pens were kept filled with bait and closed. The baiters were placed in banks and hedgerows about a hundred metres from each pen. It is surprising how uniformly dense and trackless an early winter hedgerow can appear to be, particularly when stubbles or grass give alternative routes. Equally surprising is the fact that a baiter placed in the centre of a thickly grassed bank will do its job and I had the pleasure of seeing that fifty per cent of the bait in one had gone within a few days of it being placed out while a hundred metres down the same hedgerow a fresh series of rat holes had been dug on a completely fresh site in front of a pen. From this I deduced that there had been a fair traffic down that innocent hedgerow and that while some had stopped to enjoy the bait others had hurried past to found their new colony. I think field mice attack these hedgerow baiters also but they will not persevere to open the closed sachet of bait.

The final battle came with the realisation that with all holes stopped and all systems working there was still evidence of rats within the pens. These were rats who lived within the limited cover of the pens themselves. In moving the odd bale to look for these and indeed to bait the runs beneath one saw, at the very scene of this activity, rats dead from earlier poisoning.

This is not a grossly exaggerated story although it may be a story of gross inefficiency. Everyone has heard stories of the country dweller travelling by night with the aid of a lantern who beheld a thousand twinkling lights before him and fled, expecting to be pursued, run over and devoured by an unbelievable horde of rats. In this case I believe there were such hordes moving: there are years when this happens. A few miles away a large partridge Shoot has folded and I am told that the rats there were very bad during the final year. This winter their accustomed food supply is no longer there. Not far on the other side lies a pheasant Shoot: there a professional rat catcher came for a week to clear a pen of rats which were attacking young pheasants. A magical quiet followed the few days of dead and dying rats but three or four weeks after this I was standing there waiting to pick up and I saw the grey forms busying themselves around the feeders.

I hope never to have such a year again: I do not expect I shall, and I am sure that you will not. Nevertheless I shall have my corn ready so that I can mix half a hundredweight of bait at a moment's notice. I shall have my barrier baiters in position and loaded throughout the winter to deal with the resident population and any sudden influx. I shall have a baiting point at each pen as well. One cannot but wonder what effect that will have, not on the partridge put down but on that great asset the home grown wild coveys. The rat is probably the most serious enemy faced by the partridge on our Shoot at the moment. When one sees with what speed rats find and travel to a place where food is abundant (it is said that one baiting point will attract rats within an area of twenty-five acres), one can imagine the difficulty of protecting a clutch of eggs. Not only is the rat a fierce killer – fifty pheasant poults are said to have been killed by one buck rat in one night – but he is untiring in the destruction of nests. Those rats that hasten to the pellets in the autumn are unceasingly patrolling the hedgerows in the spring.

My head keeper threw himself behind me in this matter of rat catching although his other duties prevented him acting other than as a constant spur, but in view of the fact that he had never suffered from such a plague before nor gone to such lengths to control rats he had little advice to offer save that he did once say: 'Well Geoff, if ever you meet a professional rat catcher, for goodness sake don't tell him how to catch rats.' And that, when you read this chapter, is rather apt, is it not?

I have used all sorts of poisoned baits and am prepared to use anything I can lay my hands on. Advice is less easy to come by although instructions come with each proprietary brand and from the Ministry of Agriculture. 'My word you've used more bait in three weeks than we get through in three years' said one pest officer from a large government authority. Most rats die as the book says, quickly and in their holes: the evidence of success is an unopened hole. Later in one's hedging work one comes across a few bodies. I suspect that one commercial bait is much the same as another although I like using the granulated bait which looks like a mixture of cracked wheat and millet seed, mainly because I feel that with the amount of good damp grain available at the feeders and the fact that this is arable country the rats may prefer the variety which it seems to offer. As in setting a snare one has a feeling that this or that is good but there is no real evidence to support it. The most readily available bait is good quality wheat mixed with corn oil with poison added to the makers' instructions. This I like because I know that it is fresh and because it is simple to produce in quantity.

Once the bait is made up most goes into plastic bags: 200 grms or about two trowels full. One can then tie a knot in the top of the bag, put a haversack over ones shoulder with a dozen of these plastic bags in it and walk the dogs. This will keep the baiters full but, if you are heavily engaged by the enemy, you may find it economic of time to have a separate bag of loose bait and perhaps a spade as well to deal with open holes.

I know that there are other ways of dealing with rats but they are not within my experience. I think that gassing would be expensive and the cautions with regard to the use of gas make me apprehensive. Ferreting is another method which also offers a sporting occasion and a measure of control at the end of the season where there is a modest resident population. I have never liked using my own ferrets against rats and my feeling is that as with rabbits there would always be one or two left to secure the succession. Certainly as something of a deterrent rather than as a control our pens will eventually be clothed with a six inch screen of half inch chicken wire. This is being placed around the pen bases but not secured so that the pens may be moved, should that be necessary, without heaving out the wire. Barrier baiting will continue through the summer and into next season and we hope not only to avoid the difficulties experienced this year at the pens but to give many a nesting bird the chance of rearing a brood. The terrifying and deadly onslaught of the rat is very well described in a delightful essay by Llewelyn Powys which appeared in *Country Life* on 10 September 1932 and which the reader may find, reproduced in 'BB', *The Shooting Man's Bedside Book*. To this account I commend the sceptical and the questing reader alike.

CAVE CANEM

'Sir! When I flew to seize the bird,
In spite of your command,
A louder voice than yours I heard,
And harder to withstand:
You cried – Forbear! – but in my breast
A mightier cried – Proceed!
'Twas nature, Sir, whose strong behest
Impell'd me to the deed.'
      Beau's Reply, William Cowper

Well might one sigh on reading the title to this chapter. I would myself had I the dubious pleasure of meeting this author for the first time. It seems to be the custom to say a few words about the value of the sportsman's dog, how to train and use it. That, I am not going to do. On a partridge Shoot one must beware of dogs and it takes time and experience to learn which dogs are on your side. I propose, on the other hand, to deal with the somewhat tangled web constituted by the statutes and laws which deal with dogs. The reason that I do this is that dogs can be major predators on a Shoot and it is necessary to know how to deal with them.

    People are liable in several ways for the activities of their dogs. They are liable in nuisance, that is to say liable to people, generally neighbours, for such nuisance as the continuous barking of dogs or for keeping dogs in such a way as to constitute a nuisance – for instance by reason of smell or encouragement of vermin. I am not suggesting that you should go to law in respect of any of those dogs which whine on a shoot day! So nuisance is not very likely to affect the Shoot. Owners will be liable at common law, that is to say the body of law handed down by the judges rather than that enacted by Act of Parliament, for trespass. The common law is a bit hazy about trespass by dogs. It has lingered more over the important matter of trespass by cattle now dealt with by statute. However foxhunters were held to have committed an actionable trespass in riding over a farmer's land despite his protests. Possibly an action would lie in respect of one of those householders whose property abuts on the lower part of our land and who have placed a gateway opening onto the fields for their convenience in trespassing, but I think there would have to be an actual and regular trespass following objection from the farmer and an indication of the damage being done. The remedy would be an injunction by the court forbidding repetition on pain of offending the Court. Not something to become involved in if possible: the even more awkward question of trespass by cats might come up!

Finally an owner may be liable for damage caused by his dog. The history of the growth of the law respecting this is interesting. Generally speaking owners are not liable in respect of damage caused by domestic animals. The owner of a horse which knocks you down in a field is not generally liable though now statute law has specified circumstances where he may be. The same law confirms what was already the case at common law in imputing an aura of danger to wild animals or animals not domesticated in this country. Thus it had been held that damages could be recovered where a man was bitten by a camel. On the other hand the man who tried his luck after falling off a camel due to its ungainly walk was not successful. In order to give people some protection the common law promoted the dog to a position inbetween that of a wild or dangerous animal and the purely domestic.

The dog is recognised as a friendly and domestic creature just as the cat is, to say otherwise would be to offend too many. Thus the postman who is severely scratched by a cat has no remedy. Faced with the fact that someone else's dog can be very offensive indeed the law built up a safety measure to protect people from dogs. This little invention of the common law has now been made part of statute law.

What the judges did in respect of dogs was to evolve the theory of the 'first bite'. Thus the saying that a dog is entitled to his first bite. Lawyers call this doctrine the doctrine of 'scienter' or knowledge. If the owner knew that his dog was dangerous he had to accept responsibility for it and for any injuries done by it: it was no longer just a domestic animal. If, half a century or more ago you aired your Latin by putting 'cave canem' on your gate post and thereby acquired for your property a touch of class you were half way to admitting that you knew that your dog was dangerous and I suppose that householders today who put a notice 'beware of guard dogs', because it goes with the swimming pool or the car, may also be creating difficulties for themselves.

One of the earliest cases at the end of the last century involved a dog belonging to a publican. It was bitten by another dog and likely therefore to be rabid. It was tied up by a long rope and while so tied it bit a small boy who subsequently died from rabies. The judge held that the publican was liable in law for the damage caused by the dog as he knew it to be dangerous on account of its history. The parents were awarded costs of £36 which covered the expenses to which they had been put and general damages. For a labourer who earned fourteen shillings a week, as the father did, the damages were considered generous. Rabies are not an immediate threat in this country though I have known Guns whose constancy to the bottle might have indicated a form of hydrophobia and keepers who in exasperation have exhibited symptoms of it.

I think that the Animals Act of 1971 has made the first bite doctrine a little more difficult than it was before. Section 2(2) provides:

> Where damage is caused by an animal which does not belong to a dangerous species, a keeper of the animal is liable for the damage, except as otherwise provided by this Act, if –
> (a) the damage is of a kind which the animal, unless restrained was likely to cause or which, if caused by the animal, was likely to be severe; and
> (b) the likelihood of the damage or of its being severe was due to characteristics of the animal which are not normally found in animals of the same species or are not normally so found except at particular times or in particular circumstances; and
> (c) those characteristics were known to that keeper or were at any time known to a person who at that time had charge of the animal as that keeper's servant or, where that keeper is the head of a household, were known to another keeper of the animal who is a member of that household and under the age of sixteen.

You will be very fortunate to catch even the dog that comes out every morning and eats one of your birds under this provision. So your chances of getting damages from the owner of a dog that eats your liberated partridges are virtually nil. The Animals Act does however make clear and beautiful provisions in respect of partridges in captivity. Section 3 of the Act provides as follows:

> Where a dog causes damage by killing or injuring livestock any person who is the keeper of the dog is liable for the damage except as otherwise provided by this Act.

The exception provided by the Act is in respect of livestock which has strayed on to land on which the dog rightfully was. It looks at first as if Section 3 is the answer to our prayers but livestock is defined in Section 11 as follows:

> 'Livestock' means cattle, horses, asses, mules, hinnies, sheep, pigs, goats and poultry, and also deer not in the wild state and, in Sections 3 and 9, also, while in captivity, pheasants, partridges and grouse.

You may think that all this is of no possible interest to you but it is useful to know what remedies are not available and anyhow you are no worse off than the owner of a china shop in which a bull rampaged. In fact straying cattle come under another section of the Act and it was not a bull but an ox and not a china shop but an ironmongers. It was in there for three quarters of an hour! Our Shoot did in fact ingest generously of the grain of comfort provided by Section 3 and after all the book is about our Shoot.

A young Springer dog was led astray by some partridges in the vicinity of a public footpath and, lost to its owner, after clearing the area found itself by one of our pens. With what in other circumstances one would regard as commendable dedication it jumped to the roof of the pen and forced its way through it. Of the thirty partridges placed there the day before there were left only scattered remains and a few dead bodies. A number must have escaped through the entry hole. Now an unlikely event occurred: the dog, with remarkable agility, escaped, there being a bale of straw under the place of entry and repeated his performance in a second pen. There he remained until found the next morning. The police were not very interested – they had not had the advantage of reading this book – but they did ascertain the ownership from an old address on the dog's collar. The owner put forward several defences, lack of warning signs, previous good character etc. and made a small offer. It appeared that she was covered by her household insurance and negotiations with the company in which reference was made to Section 3 resulted in our receiving a sum of £300 towards the damage done. We lost by it in terms of sport but such losses are so difficult to assess let alone to prove that we were satisfied with the result and grateful to the Act.

A magistrate's court may make an Order that a dog be kept under control or destroyed if it is adjudged to be a dangerous dog. This is a quasi criminal action that can be maintained by the police or a complaint may be taken out by a person aggrieved. Generally speaking a dog which bites or kills is considered dangerous however docile it may be at other times. Compensation will not be payable in respect of a loss and there is no fine; just the Order with costs. Although it has been held that it is not dangerous for a dog to chase rabbits and I am certain that that would normally be extended to game, Section 1 (4) of the Dogs Act, 1906, provides that when a dog is proved to have injured poultry it may be dealt with as a dangerous dog. Poultry in this case is defined by Section 87 (4) of the Animal Health Act, 1981, to include pheasant and partridge. The minister has power to make an Order the effect of which would be to exclude pheasant and partridge but he does not appear to have done so. So if you have a dog trespassing on your land under the misapprehension that he owns your sporting rights you may be able to persuade the magistrates to make an Order that he be kept under control, the more so because you can point out that in another Act liability is limited to birds in captivity and parliament has seen fit to make no such restriction here. Certainly in our case I think such an order might have been made.

It may be worth mentioning that the Dogs (Protection of Livestock) Act, 1963, makes the owner of a dog guilty of a criminal offence if it worries livestock. He becomes liable to a fine and may have to pay compensation. This Act does not apply to pheasant or partridge: in short therefore, a claim for damages may be made where a dog injures penned birds. An Order that it be kept under control may be made in respect of a dog that injures partridge at large.

At common law there is also the age old right to protect one's crops and animals from attack. Whether or not one would be justified in shooting a dog chasing or injuring partridge at large is rather a moot point. Since beaters and gamekeepers are often the policemen of a farm it is worth mentioning that Section 9 of the Animals Act, 1971, provides in addition that in civil proceedings against a person for killing or injuring a dog it shall be a defence for him to prove that he acted for the protection of livestock, that he was entitled to act for its protection and that he gave notice of the killing or of injuring the dog within forty eight hours of its occurrence to an officer in charge of a police station.

There seems to me to be a general impression that one is allowed to shoot a dog which is injuring livestock. Despite what I have said above it is not playing with words to say that that is not so. What the Act does is to provide a specific defence. In other words if you shoot a dog to protect livestock it is up to you to show that you did it in order to protect that livestock and that you had the implied or actual authority of the owner of the stock to act for the protection of that livestock. It is no good if the dog was on his way home at the time or if you have left the reporting of the matter to the police a little late.

This defence does not apply in relation to birds at liberty but it will apply in respect of partridge in captivity.

FOXES

> Tiger! Tiger! burning bright
> In the forests of the night,
> What immortal hand or eye
> Could frame thy fearful symmetry?
> *The Tiger*, Blake

As the senior vermin man on the Shoot I am constantly asked to have an all-out drive against foxes. They are my particular delight although in my ignorant and careless way I dispose of quite a few of them. So we say we will start as soon as shooting ceases: we will make an early start in February. When February comes we find we need two hundred teelers and another twenty stakes. People feel that an unemployed vermin man like me should be able to get on straight away with half a dozen iron pegs, the use of a few fencing posts and a couple of dozen wires. I do not agree and am inclined to be firm about this. I do not wish to get up before dawn and walk over two or three miles of countryside for the sake of a dozen snares. Particularly as the countryside is bisected by fences of crutch height, pig-netting and barbed wire backed by slippery and deceitful stone walls finished off with a further two or three lines of barbed wire from an earlier generation. In short the result is that we are seldom ready to start work until March.

By this time the odd corners of the large arable field of the area and such headlands as there may be bear considerable signs of the passage of fox and badger. Principally badger since he treads a well worn path. Inconveniently most of Mr Badgers' paths are a convenience to the fox also and both are great travellers. There are three phases of the snare setting operation: the first is when one is driven around by an enthusiastic head keeper who raves about what do appear to be some very good runs ('you could lose a dozen there'), the second when one lugs round a number of heavy pegs and snagging wires and finds a mere twenty or thirty usable runs, and the third is the constant pause as you go on your round struck by the sight of a run which you missed before. I do sometimes wonder if those extra runs are not made in bypassing those that have been snared. At any rate, setting a few snares on each early morning round brings your total to a worthwhile number. It is unfortunate that by this stage a number of the best runs have been fouled by catches. Not so many catches by your standards I dare say, but each in a prime position.

By this time the gentleman vermin man is really in his stride, jumping out of bed at 4 a.m. without a second's thought; when, lo and behold, green grass starts to obscure the runs. Its April again and the countryside is to become a secret place for three months with high grass and growing crops. Nothing will happen now until the corn is cut when, if the farmer has time, he will call one out to hold a gun at the end of the corn mow, a job that demands time and patience, eminently suitable for the amateur vermin man.

After harvest comes a brief period of night shooting with lights when excess rabbits and a few foxes are cleared away but as the plough gets under way opportunities for this get less. Then again the cry goes out to the vermin man to save the partridge, just three weeks blitz while the young birds are being released and finding their way round. This time the late mornings see one making acquaintance with farm workers as they come on duty and the first few days when the stakes will not go into the ground give way to dark skies and a more receptive earth.

I was very shocked the other day going on my rounds to find one of my best wires pulled tight on the neck of a pheasant. It had been a very large cock and about eight inches of thick neck bone remained below the head which had been delicately left. What upset me was that this particular snare had been set virtually in a hole in the ground: a 'killer' hole – a 'cert', situated about twelve inches from the square mesh fence and running straight down into the ground under the fence and out the other side in a declivity there, a foot or more below the fence level and within a wood. What right had a cock pheasant to be using that route? He was, as I say, a very large one and a wild one: no doubt he knew every route and short cut in that area of the farm.

While established crossings and underpasses are opened up each year, routes themselves vary. There was a magnificient one in the spring which came under a square mesh fence fixed to wooden cross bars which had been erected by the gas board in the course of some of their work. I had a wire a few feet from the underpass set well up to avoid badgers. It caught nothing but was so obviously a 'killer' that I left the stake in situ. This autumn the underpass was closed and overgrown when I started my rounds but one morning it was opened up: not only that but paved, signposted and very nearly lit! Alas the path now ran a foot or more to one side of its former course. Another lesson for me!

In the spring a suitable place for a snare lay at the top of a chalk digging where a few yards of rough grass bounded the plough. It was unproductive and when I went there in the autumn the hedge to one side was dense and unbroken and the grass above the cutting was uniform save where it had been crushed by a turning tractor. Within two weeks my head keeper had found three partridge dead in a release pen and it was obviously the work of a fox which had entered through the fox-grid (the birds had returned to jug.) With considerable skill he tracked the fox across newly sown ground which had been subjected to torrential rain and so bore footprints for the five hundred yards or more of the fox's journey. The prints led to my chalk cutting. In the grass there were feathers and a regular railway junction of tracks. After raising a number of objections relating to time, material and the length of my present round I was sent off to deal with the incursion in the usual way. An unfortunate aspect of this particular site was that to deal with the runs one had to advance to the centre of the area and having thrown pegs, teelers and snagged wires fairly liberally around and found some substantial rocky sub-strata in the course of my hammering, the whole area looked like a battlefield. It was gratifying therefore to find a very small vixen waiting there on the second morning after the setting.

Now my question is, and I am not knowledgeable in these matters, was it the little vixen who made all those runs where before there had been nothing? Was it a couple of nights work or would she perhaps have entertained there? Of course those runs were completely effaced but I am inclined to believe that a run is fairly quickly made and maintained with a modicum of use until the growth of grass obliterates everything.

An effective way of clearing foxes as they come in, and keep coming in as they will, is to poison them. This means putting poison in carcases of rabbits or other meat and leaving it as with rats where domestic animals will not get at it. Poison will kill a lot of things besides foxes: it is not selective. Now the use of poison is illegal though there are exceptions in respect of rats, mice and small ground vermin while parliament may and I believe has made exceptions in the case of coypu and squirrels. Even these exceptions are subject to the nature of the poison used.

We do not of course use poison and the reason that I mention it is that so many people do not realise what the alternative to snaring, shooting and hunting is. Should rabies ever gain a foothold in this country and it be sought to clear a particular area of foxes then I do not see what method other than the use of poison could be used to achieve that result. We snare actively and we also shoot with lights at night.

Shooting in that way is an adjunct to snaring but there is only a limited period when one can drive a vehicle on the fields. Particularly near towns shooting from a vehicle involves a good deal of preparation if one is to warn all the people who may become aware of lights being used on or near their land. While we do have some success from shooting at night it is not a precise science nor as rewarding as a good foray over your land at cub hunting time by the local hunt. They had five cubs in one day around our area which I reckon is the equivalent of two week's hard labour with snares. Nor do their victims suffer the agony of poison, or snare or of festering wound. Unfortunately our proximity to a built up area and the incidence of lambing limits the help we obtain from the hunt.

I frequently seek out the fox with a .22 rifle. Such a rifle is not suitable for anything much over seventy paces but within that range it is humane and effective when properly used. I never take a standing shot: I use, I have to use, a telescopic sight and a sound moderator. I like to go out at first light in the summer and with my quiet gun I can bring back a rabbit or two without rousing the neighbourhood. That is a good time to see what is on the land whether it be the regular line of four badgers returning to their set by their habitual route after a survey of the village gardens or a hen pheasant and her chicks crossing a track. This is the time one begins to know the one or two wild coveys. The foxes which I see in the early mornings are my friends: they know me and I know them. Generally I see one sitting on the side of Greenhill as I come round it. I view him carefully with my field glasses and then make a long, carefully prepared stalk. When I crawl over the selected rise I often see my fox watching me from the vantage point I have just vacated.

I have a terrible confession to make, not perhaps such a surprise coming from an incompetent such as myself. I did not shoot a single fox last year. I met two face to face: the first I squeaked up having seen him first and put myself in a comfortable position below a crest. He came fast and slightly to one side of me. Normally the fox stops in surprise at this point: this fox slowed but kept on. As he was determined not to stop I decided to take a moving shot – unusual for me. He was not twenty paces off sliding off the crest: I squeezed the trigger but no shot – I had left the safety catch on. I stood up and surveyed the whole of the hillside before me – there was no fox; these wonderful animals are able to disappear at will. On a second occasion I saw a fox quartering in my direction a hundred and fifty yards off. I got down at once and crawled to a little mound; as I slowly gained the top I was horrified to find myself face to face with the fox who had run up to find what sort of injured animal was dragging itself towards him. I had no time to utter more than a word of apology before he was away up the hillside. How bitter in those circumstances to learn that a member of the Shoot out walking with a shotgun had come upon and shot one of my foxes while it lay sleeping in the mid-day sun secure in the knowledge that no approach would be made without the usual courtesies!

Unlaid hedges, kept to a minimum height by a mechanical cutter, slowly decay. In some cases our hedges are but isolated growth along the barbed wire fences. In these circumstances there are innumerable crossing places for foxes and snaring is difficult. The fox that uses these hedges as a general line of march, walking alongside them, is more likely to be a victim but the changing surface of the ground as the plough follows the combine leaves little growth for a run to show up in. What we have done in such a case and what we hope to do more of is to place a few yards of sheep netting through the fence, angled so as to direct the wanderer towards the hedge. Near the hedge and on each side of it an artificial run is created under the wire. We have not yet had regular use made of our decoy. One of our unanswered questions is how do you stop a snared fox from ruining such a set up? I know that someone will say, 'Use a log to anchor the wire', but for us logs are out.

We used a lot of Renardine round the pens last season. How effective it was is difficult to say. Certainly the vixen who entered one of the release sections thought nothing of it.

For us foxes will always remain the subject of hard work. One hopes that fresh and energetic and indeed younger vermin men will come forward to take on this task as each last one tires. One can be secure in the knowledge that the foxes will keep coming. Apart from plenty of cliff-side cover near by, the built up areas which nearly surround us are a wonderful breeding ground. Our very best efforts will do no more than allow a modest breeding stock of partridge and a healthy head of foxes.

THE WORKING PARTY

> He had a large map representing the sea
> Without the least vestige of land
> And the crew were much pleased when they found it to be
> A map they could all understand.
> 'What's the good of Mercator's North Pole and Equators,
> Tropics, Zones and meridian lines?'
> So the Bell man would cry and the crew would reply:
> 'They are merely conventional signs.'
> *The Hunting of the Snark*, Lear

I suppose that our working party is a story in itself. Not one that is much likely to interest the reader perhaps and a matter which itself could cause more dissension than cohesion on many Shoots. Nevertheless it is an integral part of our Shoot, a useful forum for ideas as well as a method of binding the members together in a sense of comradeship and achievement. It is also a very necessary body for us as we have no full time staff and a great deal of work to do.

The working party, which is in effect the second syndicate, is at work all the year, its ear to the ground, picking up discarded items. It is a principle of theirs that everything can be fixed somewhere, somehow: everything done by someone or their friend. Even so there are things beyond our reach but if they are marketed then we may have the money for them as a result of our success elsewhere. Farmers and of course those connected with the Shoot are always very kind to us. Only today my head keeper was telling me how he had rung up a Shoot member who agreed to let him have sixty sheets of very good corrugated iron: 'I generally charge a pound a sheet for it' he said, 'What will you offer?' 'Why nothing at all of course,' said my head keeper. 'In that case you had better take it on,' said our friend. 'Well, its not as simple as that,' said my head keeper. 'You realise we shall need your pick-up to transport it?' 'I just hope I don't get any more calls like yours tonight,' replied the donor. Five gallon drums are in great demand: we need upwards of sixty on the Shoot and they do not have a very long life. Farmers and large authorities do not always have a use for the containers that flow into

A Working Party. *Paul Middleton*

their undertakings – we do. Large forty five gallon drums are very valuable to us. Even when they have been painted the bottoms and the tops steadily rust out. Five gallon metal drums are prizes indeed, becoming very hard to find. Corrugated iron can be picked out of tht treasure chest the farm dump. Rolls of wire lie there abandoned. Torn sheep netting has uses either as a guide to foxes wandering the hedgerows or as a foxproof base for pens. Old stakes can be recovered and put to many uses. Fortunately we are not bothered by squirrels and plastic drums will meet our needs next year. We have to prepare drums for the whole Shoot next year in order to dispense the tailings with which we are going to feed the birds. Each feeder will have its corrugated iron shelter over it.

The working party are a mixed lot: the lawyer, the gunsmith and the fisherman work side by side. Did you know that the powerful springs of a hay tedder, snapped off and rusting under the bank can be forged into first class gun springs? There is a blacksmith who can operate power tools from the compressor on the back of his Land Rover and a carpenter. They can do with ease and exactitude those little jobs in the pens that one finds so difficult to plan let alone execute. Finally there is a sprinkling of men who, unlike me, are blessed with a straight eye, whose work stands out even when it comes to digging a straight sided ditch let alone putting a post in upright. We do lack an electrician and I have wasted a lot of time pouring water on the base of an electric fencer and doing strange things to its internal workings while cursing the lack of a competent colleague. Of course we can call in aid from the farm workshop but we do try to be independent. So, if you see an advertisement for an electrician, a good safe shot, for a small Shoot, you will know that it is our syndicate that has taken this sensible step towards self-sufficiency.

As every full time keeper knows to his cost there is very little time in which to do much of the necessary work on a Shoot. Two great events eclipse our life. First of all the shooting season itself with its urgent build up, extending virtually from the harvest until February, precludes a body of men descending on the fields. Secondly the crops, already springing in February, quickly grow and prohibit trespass.

This year we have banked up a hundred and twenty yards of one of our main hedges and laid it for that distance. We have made a start on a second hedge. We hope to complete the whole length of the first hedge over a period of three years providing a solid bank with good nesting cover above. The whole of the bank and verge have been given a scattering of dung to encourage rank growth. In the few weeks between the first of February and the opening of the first buds it is a race against time. We work for three or four hours of a Sunday morning and find that quite enough. Indeed I think that a steady programme of banking and hedge laying might soon find a few gaps in the volunteer ranks!

As spring gets underway we have to set up gallows for the feeders and erect the shelters above. As we have had the great good fortune to have been given the wood for the considerable number of stakes needed for the job, these have first to be sharpened and creosoted. On top of this the pens have to be set to rights, straw bales removed and disposed of and fresh provision made for the new season. Each year we heave a sigh of relief and see our permanent pens and their accoutrements duly set out in the knowledge that next year there will only be the finishing touches to add. Just as is the case every year, we find now that there are two pens to be moved a considerable distance on top of all the other work.

We cannot afford to destroy any of the brushwood removed from the hedge: it all has to be dragged off to provide cover and nesting sites elsewhere. We are fortunate in having some strong sons to help in this work. It would be much more companionable to have the hedge cutter's bonus of a roaring bonfire before which to take our break. A number of well rooted cuttings of lonicera have been planted in bare places where, willing though that shrub is, they will have to fight to survive in the bare chalk. Already five hundred cuttings have been set to produce a line of hedge at one of the flushing points next year. If we are lucky it will provide a nucleus from which, reinforced by further contributions, a hedge may eventually take shape. It may be worth describing the simple method used in propagating the plants for our hedgerows, something we try to do in March. The rooting compost is earth fortified with moss peat for about a third of its volume and a few shovels full of coarse sand, if available, to every barrow load. This composition having been mixed and left to absorb rain for a day or two is then pressed into a number of half drums. Slips of lonicera or hawthorn three to four inches in length and torn from their junction with the parent plant are trimmed at the bottom with a sharp knife, dipped in water and then into a rooting compound and stuck into the compost with the help of a six inch nail. The container with about thirty cuttings in it is then slipped into a polythene bag the ends of which are tucked under and the whole then placed in a cool greenhouse for six weeks. At the moment I rejoice to have eight half drums of cuttings securely contained within one of the polythene sacks that form an inner lining to the large fertiliser bags now used on many farms. Then the containers are removed from within the polythene and placed outside in a shady place to harden off for a day or two. Finally the cuttings are transplanted into individual polythene pots containing a light soil. Left in a shady place well grown plants each with its ball of soil can be eased out of their containers and planted during any wet period probably the following autumn or spring. We try to plant about 1 ft 6 in apart in two rows about one foot apart. A good mulch of manure if it is available finishes the operation.

It is a good thing that time for the more arduous labour is short. There is a limit to the burden that enthusiasm can bear. Once the heavy work finishes in March or April individual members of the syndicate add their personal contributions throughout the year.

Ours is a puny labour in a great countryside but in the acres around us there are not so many laid hedges and not many new planted ones. I expect that the cattle and occasionally a deer or hare will dispose of many of the plants in the course of the summer but it is a start. Hawthorn has a limited life and the mechanical cutter keeps each bush trimmed so that there is very little propagation, the barbed wire fence serves the purpose better. It seems to me that unless it is replaced artifically a lot of the pedigree hawthorn will die out. Planting is the alternative to allowing the bush to grow and later laying it and banking up. That is probably true of a number of hedgerow species but it is not so of the blackthorn. That plant spreads insidiously and propagates itself by sucker and thus is well adapted to hard cutting by machine. Indeed the mechanical cutter can provide and maintain a very good hedge of blackthorn. In awkward corners the bush even produces an abundance of fruit to satisfy those who have a purpose for it (and very grateful to that mellowed and fortified fruit have I been on sundry wet and tiring days). Those hedges are probably the more natural for this sort of countryside providing in such circumstances good nesting cover.

It is pleasant to be one of the beaters who comprise our syndicate at the start of a season and see, as one hopes, the orderly pens and feeders, the prepared hedge with its purpose built tunnels and passes for man and beast and to observe the growth here and the failure there, enjoying a creator's pride in that harmony which nature is prepared to produce with so slight attention on our part to the notes.

POSTSCRIPT

> Very few, even of our common birds, are more generally known than the Partridge. From the first of September to the first of February, in large towns, every poulterer's shop is pretty sure to be decorated with a goodly array of these birds.
> British Birds and their Haunts, Rev. C. A. A. Johns

Time does not stand still while one writes. Such time as one has is rapidly absorbed in the work of the coming season and writing suffers in consequence. So it is that I find myself rather to my surprise in the middle of another shooting season and perhaps a little more experienced an observer than when I started. What is there to show for the experiences of last year? Quite a lot of things that were to have been done have not been done or have been done only in part. For the efforts that have been made some results are to hand.

First of all we have had on our Shoot what is said to have been the best season for wild birds that has been known for the past ten years and memory goes not beyond that. We have noted twenty coveys ranging from a record of fifteen Greys down to little one chick who had the misfortune to be shot on the first day – my head keeper claims to have recognised it, an Ogridge! We have had wild coveys of Greys and we have had Ogridges. A hundred birds all together we believe and there are wild birds on the perimeters as well.

We did not manage to tag the birds as we had hoped and in the end we failed to make our release and holding pens interchangeable by building additional fox-grids. As we have had good weather we have had no cause to bemoan that fact.

FEEDERS

Our supply of tailings or cleanings turned out to be small corn with little or no weed content. As a result the Owen Tickler feeders were not a great success. Not unnaturally the small grains tended to be hammered out by the birds. We have found that these feeders are an awful nuisance to fill, requiring two men and a funnel for the best results! Had we been filling them with cleanings containing a much greater proportion of chaff then the labour of filling would have been even greater but the drums would have been much lighter when filled and easier therefore to hang. We are already experimenting with the new feeder, the McDonald feeder. So far every feeder described in this book has been fine for one purpose or in one set of circumstances. I do not include among those the Game Conservancy's letter box feeder as this has not been the subject of trial. The Mcdonald feeder has faults. Too great a weight of feed depresses the plastic insert, the lips rise and the rain enters. Too fine a feed and it runs down the side of the plastic insert. So we place a second piece of plastic across the first and use a rag or tissue to prevent the grain running down the side. A good, close fitting circle can be obtained from the bottom of a round plastic drum if you have drums to spare. To give ourselves leeway we have enlarged the hole in the plastic insert to something about three inches in diameter and placed a short length of three inch plastic drainpipe in the centre of the second piece of plastic. Now the height of the plastic insert in the drum is no longer critical and by raising or lowering the plastic pipe (kept in place by friction) we can deal with slow or fast flowing feed. That is why a piece of rag makes a better sealant than say, a length of sticky tape. It is easy to take the plastic out to adjust the height of the piping.

We have a number of these feeders set out at the pens where they are guarded from badgers by electric fences. A generous collar inside the neck of each drum ensures that it holds the maximum quantity and baler twine runs from the centre bottom up through the feed pipe to the cross bar of the shelter – that prevents the drum being blown over. It may still prove necessary to put a couple of wires under the inserts to prevent them bending under a weight of corn: time will tell. The aim, of course, is to use a metal drum once our teething troubles are over.

FOOD

Although we did not obtain the sort of tailings we had anticipated, the small corn we used was set on at once by the birds introduced to the pens and above all, taken by birds long released. I should like to say that it was taken by the wild coveys: I anticipate that it was but I have no evidence at all to that effect. A little hard weather and we shall see! The birds which we have shot have been well nourished and the crops

Food and shelter provided; peace secured by an electric fence

of most contained our small corn. I do not think we shall ever feed quality wheat again.

ELECTRIC FENCES

We have used five electric fences this season, a very expensive outlay although we were able to get them second hand. Two consisted of electrified sheep netting and three were of a couple of lines of live wire. It took some time to work out how best to use the sheep netting which was too long for the purpose and how best to set it up. It involves more work than a double wire and I found it less easy to maintain. That is to say a wider swathe through the growth surrounding the pens seems to be necessary and maintaining a bare, or a relatively bare, surface beneath the sheep netting is more awkward. A double or treble wire, the bottom line being an earth, is easier to keep clear of shorting weed and easy to step over. We lost one bird which became entangled in the sheep netting where it had been doubled round. It is difficult to assess the success of the fences because we had little interference at any of our pens, but we enjoyed great peace of mind as a result of their use. In fact it is possible to make a comparison. In a pen which had previously suffered interference we now had none, but some three weeks after the electric wire ceased to be active, because the batteries had not been replaced, a fox sat at the entrance to the release pen and disposed of several birds. Two of our pen fences were operated on car batteries, three by dry batteries. We found that the car batteries which are heavy and cumbersome and liable to flood one's transport with acid when overturned suited us much better than the dry batteries. When the latter fail one is never entirely cetain of the reason and the quartermaster is likely to tell one to return and pour water round the earth again. With the car batteries one simply fits a recharged battery and the thing springs to life. As the batteries which we place in plastic drums are never moved save for recharging we do not face the problem of regular movement of a cumbersome object which must tell against them in farm use. We hope to increase our use of electric fencing.

THE BIRDS

The weather this year has been kind to us. A few days of rain and storm drives us to despair but overall we have had nothing to complain about. Rats have persisted pretty well everywhere but have been repulsed without loss and without leaving any shaming evidence of their appearance. It is sufficient to say that we have had to go round the pens more frequently with our bait bag than to replenish the hoppers. Other vermin have fallen to traps and those that have survived have not been a cause for concern. The buzzard perches heavily on the top of the release pen and his large droppings fall to the inner shelter. At first we wondered at an animal large enough to produce such evidence of a visit and yet able to pass through the fox-grids! Was someone playing a joke? A few circles of smeared feathers have remained to show where foxes pass but it has been a season when we could well afford a few foxes. Thus there are and have been sufficient birds walking about ahead of one or taking off in long glides to be in themselves quite a worry, who or what else would notice these promenading birds. We were glad from that point of view when the first shoot achieved its sixty birds. The three shoots of the first syndicate averaged just over sixty birds each although the wind was against us on the first two. The balance of birds and weather was such that each shoot accounted for about sixty birds. On the last shoot there were enough birds shown to give rise to much discussion both as to those which had passed unscathed and those that formed the good number of birds left on the Shoot afterwards. This was not for want of cartridges fired at them! A large number of birds went over the Guns and they were fine, strong birds, high birds. I think the beaters were lined up, as I could see through my glasses, a quarter of a mile away when the first covey of wild Greys came over at speed on each of the first two drives the first syndicate had on their last day. Only fourteen Greys were released for the first syndicate in circumstances which I shall relate later but with the several wild coveys which passed over the Guns in the course of their three days shooting a total bag of four Greys by the first syndicate might seem to be disappointing. For me it was a great pleasure. Insignificant and small in comparison with other partridge Shoots as ours may be, to have taken part in showing first class birds to good shots on three occasions and to be left with the greater part of the stock is to me as great a distinction as I could wish for. To have the Guns talking about those that came over the top of the pylon wires or which travelled down the line to escape unscathed was the success that all who took part in raising and showing the birds sought. It was very satisfying as one cleared up after the last day of the first syndicate to see the odd small covey making its way back home and upon opening the anti fox-grids to have birds almost queuing at each pen to get back (The grids are closed before each shoot.) That does raise the questions of whether the birds become too tied to their release pens and whether their natural way of life is thus interfered with to too great an extent. At the moment I say the answer is 'No!' and I say it because these are birds which can fly, we think, as strongly as any other and they are birds which do fly when driven, fly high, are shot at and return. What more do you want?

RED-LEGS AND GREYS

I have said that we only released fourteen Greys for the first syndicate. In fact, following their last shoot and prior to the start of the second syndicate's season, twelve more have been put down. Instead of releasing twenty-five or thirty Greys into the swedes as we normally do, this year we released twenty-five Red-legs or Ogridges and eight Greys at one pen and thirty-five Red-legs or Ogridges and six Greys at another pen which we call Mid Fossil Fence. The latter is a part of the conurbation of pens towards the centre of the Shoot while the former, in the swedes, is a temporary single pen which follows the root crop each season. The pen in the swedes tends to be isolated from the rest of the Shoot. These birds, Red-legs and Greys, were said to have been brought up together as one species and the object was that we should see for ourselves the effect of such a mix which has been the subject of experiment by others and the subject of an article in *The Shooting Times* and *Country Magazine*. The aim is to form a covey of the mixed species so that when they run in the stubbles the Red-legs take the Greys with them and when the Greys seek shelter in the swedes the Greys take the Red-legs with them. I should have liked to have started my observations in the rearing pens and in particular to have discovered to what extent the composition of the coveys was attended by chance. For instance were the original two batches once one with the top up batch which we received later? Were the birds in each of our pens from a separate rearing pen or drawn from a larger batch of the mixed species? I do not know since I am, as you will be aware, more of a casual observer than an investigative reporter. I was shocked to learn, for instance, that when the callers are removed from various pens near the centre of the Shoot before a shooting day they are kept and later replaced without strict regard to their pen of origin: presumably on the basis that all Chinamen are alike! A sad blow to all theory of covey forming although not so devastating as it may sound since a small number of pens, those liable to interference alone, are concerned and the chances are that most of the birds will find themselves replaced in their original pen when the day is done.

At any rate the results of our trial have been very interesting. The Greys in both pens seemed to live very much their own lives, not as a clique but as individuals unconcerned with the Red-legs. The single Grey among the Red-legs would push inconsequentially past them in the never ceasing search for an exit: faster and more intelligent – wilder perhaps? The great distinction perhaps was that the Greys lived on the ground, the Red-legs on the tops of the shelters. The Greys came to the top of the shelter when there were other Greys in the release section of the pen but did not, generally, spend much time there. Once a pophole was opened the Greys would be first out and indeed if one of their number remained behind for some reason then the same Greys would be the first back!

The mixture of Greys and Red-legs were placed in the two pens on 24 September and after some bad weather a first release was made six days later on 30 September. Four Greys were kept in each holding pen with about half the original number of Red-legs. We kept this balance in the pens for another week and then released most leaving two Greys and two Red-legs in the swedes as callers and four Red-legs at Mid Fossil

Fence. The four Red-legs were left in exasperation because even with the convenience of a closed release pen the difficulty of keeping back just two Greys or of returning just two Greys proved too much to an indolent scribe! The answer must be to catch your two Greys and then shepherd the other birds out but the slightest squeak from the one in your hand will bring back those already in the release section.

There is a distinction between the pens at Mid Fossil Fence and the swedes which I have already mentioned. One is a double pen with a release section and a holding section and the other which is in the swedes is a single pen. In the double pen at Mid Fossil Fence there always seemed to be birds in the release section: yes they did fly but generally in two sections. First of all those outside the pen, Red-legs and Greys, would fly off. They would fly off raggedly and would not necessarily land in the same immediate area. The reason was that the balance of the covey was lying low in the release section. They would wait until the last moment and then take off raggedly through the fox-grids and fly down towards the Shoot centre. Sometimes I would go to that pen and particularly when the weather was bad there would be no sign of a bird. As I went about my business sounds of panic would arise from the release pen and bird after bird would fly against the netting, scurry from the release grids and away. On more than one such occasion I have then visited a pen at the bottom of the hill to see Greys and Red-legs in the release section there. On one of the first syndicate Shoots the person whose duty it was to see that release pens were empty and the grids shut found the covey so unwilling to leave that he left it there. That beat was not in the event driven and the birds remained there throughout the day!

So the lesson of Mid Fossil Fence was that the birds stayed really tight when brought up together and on the whole stayed together. Secondly that they seemed to be as well held by callers comprising Red-legs as by Greys. In the first lay the great advantage of the mixture: they were a steadfast covey. It is difficult to compare them with the birds of the year before because those birds had not had such favourable conditions. Certainly there was no comparison in staying power. Nor did those of the previous year fly so well when disturbed.

At the swedes it was another story of success. The second release left two Red-legs and two Greys who remained in the pen until the first syndicate ceased shooting – in fact until 18 November. The pen was on tussocky grass in a small stubble field adjoining the swedes and the swedes were intersown with low kale. Thus the birds had stubble, rough grass and roots. Because there was no release section the released birds remained an undivided covey throughout. One could count them most mornings. I presumed that when they were not visible in the stubble they were in the swedes but that was rare. At first they were always close to the pen. On one occasion when no birds were there I found an outside feeder empty. I filled it and on returning from the car with something I required I saw bird after bird slip from the food shelter through the adjoining hedge. For such short and simple pleasures one works the day long!

Those Red-legs hardly ever ran: they took off as a covey, a large thundering covey. On the first Shoot day we were worried lest we could not blank them into the swedes. They rose nevertheless from the swedes just over the rise from the beaters and sped in formation over the Guns – I think two came down. A wild covey of seven Greys from the same field also left the swedes. One of these was brought down but flew on strongly afterwards. Two days later I noticed that there were only six in that covey. On the second Shoot the released birds rose in a great body before the beaters and swept over the crest towards the Guns at the valley edge. We heard nothing and were disappointed but afterwards the Guns told us that the birds had flown magnificently and again two were down. Could the covey be brought back? The answer was 'No'. They had been seen to land about a quarter of a mile away. Should we see them again? The following morning a strong covey of eighteen flew from the stubbles into the swedes!

On the last Shoot the covey rose erratically from the swedes and suffered casualties in consequence. Two days after on 22 November there were five Greys near the pen peering at me from the swedes. I presumed that the Red-legs were behind them. However, when I went into rough ground at the other end of the stubbles up got a covey of twelve Red-legs. It seemed that the species had gone their natural ways at last – the Greys to the swedes and the Red-legs to the stubbles and rough grass. Both were still within easy reach of the original release pen. Subsequently both at the swedes and at Mid Fossil Fence one saw odd mixes. 'That's odd,' said a visiting Gun, 'there were ten Red-legs and one Grey in that covey' – and there were other mixes.

What are we to gather from all this? Well, I do not pretend to enough knowledge to pontificate. What appeals to me is the strength of the group at the swedes, both its strength in flight and its compact form as a covey. Had I kept better notes I could have said: 'Yes, they shot so many and the wastage was so much.' One has always wanted to know to what

A Grey with the Red-legs

extent pricked birds account for the diminution of numbers. The Guns on our Shoot are, I am told, good shots and my friend Tim says that a good shot does much more harm than a bad one because a good shot never misses by much and so the wastage is greater.

The other thing about the release at the swedes is that it produced a large covey, predominantly of Red-legs which flew immediately. Not only did it fly when alarmed but it flew into the swedes. Generally speaking Red-legs are said not to fly into cover. When they are in a good mood you can get them to run into it: these would fly into it. Up to this point you can say that we have only established a covey with the characteristics of a covey of Greys. Their final asset was that they stuck to their ground like Red-legs and it is there that the great advantage of a mixed covey seems to lie. We know that Greys are territorial but just try coming to terms on more than two occasions with a covey released on our land! The year before I think we released about thirty Greys in the swedes. They stuck close to their callers for the first week or so but after the first Shoot they were off!

'What did the Greys contribute to the bag?' I hear you ask. It is a question that always crops up. It is no good saying that all the Guns ran out of cartridges or that they had a splendid day. 'How many birds did you get?' Someone got a right and left at very high Greys from Mid

Fossil Fence on the first Shoot. It was a misfortune which left us two short. Apart from that they kept their numbers up to the end. 'No wonder' you say 'that they were prepared to stay!' It is true that the first syndicate shot two or three more but we decided they were from wild coveys. Other released Greys fell to the second syndicate.

There is no doubt in our minds that the mix produced a hard holding, hard flying covey and it would probably improve the Shoot though greatly increase the work if all the birds were mixed. There may be more work to do on the proportions of the mix but we took the figures we were given and they seemed to work out well. You will remember, I am sure, that these birds are not first mixed when put in the release pen but birds which have been brought up together.

CONCLUSION

> 'And everybody praised the Duke
> Who this great fight did win.'
> 'But what good came of it at last?'
> Quoth little Peterkin:
> 'Why that I cannot tell,' said he,
> 'But 'twas a famous victory.'
> *After Blenheim,* Robert Southey

CONSERVATION

'I do believe that that's the first sparrow hawk I've seen here for twenty years,' said the owner of Glebe Farm as we saw the bird flit over the hedge from the pens. One cannot see a sparrow hawk among the partridge without mixed feelings. The buzzard appears each autumn sitting on a fence post looking ill. Perhaps he is injured? At your approach he lumbers heavily off. He gets a share in what is going: for many birds the partridge are a lifeline. It is true that a winter wood where game is not preserved is a cold and silent place but once the feeders are put round for the pheasants everything turns up. The place resounds with music. Out on the downs those that do not eat partridge live off the food left for partridge. Since our pens are scattered around there is food for all, good and bad but mostly, I think, good. One of the good things about shooting pheasants is the pleasure one gets from watching the various birds and animals slip out of the wood in front of the beaters. A deer may break in front of you, occasionally an owl is hustled involuntarily from his shadowed seclusion. Other birds flit a few trees in advance of the beaters. On a partridge Shoot, on our partridge Shoot at any rate, there is not much to enliven the long wait before the first birds come over but in terms of conservation a very much larger area is given over to wild life. There is food, cover and limited protection against vermin.

For most of the Guns partridge shooting is a great interest, an excitement like all good sport, leaving the sportsman with an occasional triumph but more often the memory of chances missed, of uncertainty, the failure to pick out the bird of his choice and follow through. For the

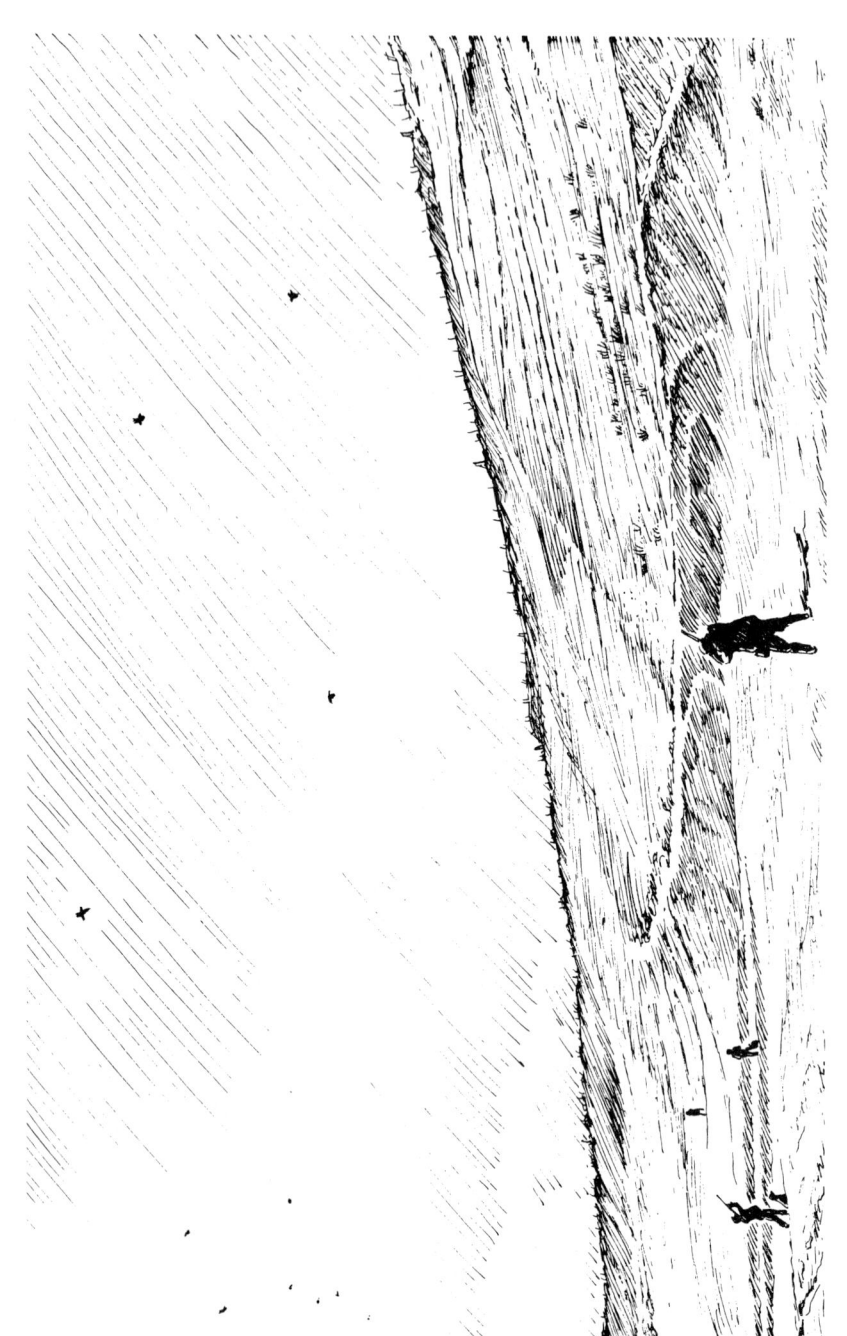

The long wait . . . is over. *From a photograph by Paul Middleton*

partridge it is a disturbance which comes two or three times in the season and although he will not hesitate to leave the area unless it holds strong attractions for him, it is my opinion that he has little idea what it is all about, either he registers it as one of the hundred and one inconveniences he will seek to avoid in future or he goes to the larder in prime condition having led a comparatively pampered and certainly happy existence up to that point. For my part partridge shooting has no great appeal but I do think that showing partridge for sport is a most demanding occupation, a most satisfying one and one which seems to combine every facet of conservation as I see it: from encouraging the growth of coarse weed, to laying hedges and to populating a countryside with every living creature. There is a covey of ten young Red-legs – not Greys – Red-legs, down at the bottom of Fossil. On approach one flew, a little bumble bee. He flew right across the valley and two minutes later missed his siblings and flew back. That is enough to keep me happy for a long while.

HELP FROM THE COMMUNITY

I think it is relevant for me to pay tribute in respect of the great kindness we have received in running the Shoot from as many people who are not connected with the Shoot as from those who are. I have already mentioned the method by which we acquired a great deal of corrugated iron and there are other instances. In my search for stakes for the feeder shelters I was dismayed to find a shortage of the sort of small or sub-standard stake I needed. I explained our position to the general who does a good deal of forestry work and he thought that he might have sufficient trimmings and odd lengths to meet our needs. Diffidently I hesitated to accept his offer, I am but a small cog in a business with very little capital and I raised the question of price. 'Oh I don't think the estate would want to make any charge for this,' he replied. The adjoining farm from which I borrow odd things lent me an angle grinder. 'You had better take on half a dozen blades,' said Simon. 'That's all right, we buy them in bulk and I expect we get them much cheaper than you would.'

We have had a great deal of help from many people. All in all there is strong support for the sporting life of the countryside from those who neither shoot nor hunt as from those who do. When one hears criticism of the sporting world emanating mainly from urban society one is reminded, is one not, of the sincere efforts of missionaries in foreign lands whose first thought was to clad the natives decently and whose second thought was to train them to ways alien to their culture and incompatible with the circumstances in which they lived.

THE GREAT WILD COUNTRY!

I suppose that my description of our Shoot is such that if you came across a green and pleasant land dotted with pens and pairing birds you would say: 'I recognise that; it's a sort of arcadia fashioned by a body of intrepid workers who call themselves "the second syndicate".' Well! If that is the impression I have given, it is wrong. Despite our efforts the land is bare. Bare in winter: an unbelievable jungle in the summer. Our planted hedge will droop in the summer heat. The rain wil restore our bank to a more natural level. In a year or so somebody will suggest moving the pens and working the whole Shoot on a new basis. Perhaps a bird watching conservancy? Foxes even now prowl the outskirts awaiting the sign that our puny efforts are wasting. It is the soil that calls the tune and we make little impression on it. Like the small allotment one has passed each day with admiration, its rows immaculate, its surface mulched – the machinery of the garden, the butts, the compost heap and the frame the evidence of its worth – all to be replaced after a year's neglect by a level sward seemingly no more fertile than the neighbouring ground.

FINIS

This can be no conclusion though it may be an incompetent beginning. The best I can do is to end and one hopes that a more definitive work will eclipse this. If there is a lacuna in published works dealing with this aspect of the life of the partridge then it is no more than is to be expected when so much is changing, as has ever been the case with them.

What we have done is to exert ourselves in a harmless endeavour, well, perhaps something a little better than that. We release birds where there are few and of those released we take a third or a quarter. Those we take have had a better life than the supermarket chicken. They have known the pleasure of the morning dew and the warmth of the midday sun. They have answered the distant call of a mate and enjoyed the excitement of danger. Those that were left have had a good start. They have perhaps survived, perhaps fallen in nature's great cycle providing food and ensuring survival for others. Nature is never kind but they have led a natural life. Above all there are partridge on the downs.

And what about the downs? Nature has done well out of this. The stubbles have fed flocks of feral and a few wood pigeon. Where else will you see stubble round about? One has seen the heavy buzzard rise slowly from the field and on approaching seen the rooks fly off and last of all the magpies. All from the carcase of one bird which has met death through some misadventure. Vast flocks of finches have feasted on the stubbles. Small birds frequent the feeders through the winter. The badgers know where to come in time of need. For the wild life it has been a conservation area as all Shoots are to a greater or lesser extent.

The second syndicate have enjoyed their sport but playing to win has not been the name of the game. One has the odd bird to remember through the year and several to be reminded of. The shooting has not been a major part of the enterprise. Building up the Shoot has been a labour of love but one which has largely had to carry its own reward. No sooner does a season start with its constant attendance on the birds than the time to plan for next year is at hand. Those vital few weeks from February on when one can get on the land and do this and do that are succeeded by a very short space of time before the birds are ordered and the whole routine starts again. The work has to be its own reward, the birds are paid for in cash.

I told my head keeper the other day that a rational approach would be for him to do a few evening's work decorating or what you will on a casual basis and with the earnings of two or three week's work he could buy a Gun on a Shoot where everything was provided by nature, but he would have none of it.

It is something to have assisted nature a little, to have a few birds in the freezer; a harvest to fill out that of the blackberries, more rarely mushrooms, pigeon hard won in season, a few rabbits and to have walked many miles over the hills before resting with a sense of health and well being.

BIBLIOGRAPHY

'BB', *The Shooting Man's Bedside Book* (1986) The Boydell Press, Woodbridge

Bonnett Frank, *The Pageant of Nature vol.2, British Wild Life and its Wonders* (1923) Cassell PC, London

Coles Charles, *The Complete Book of Game Conservation* (2nd edn 1975) Barrie and Jenkins Ltd, London

Delacour Dr Jean, *Pheasant Breeding and Care* (5th edn 1978) TFH Publications Ltd

Drought J. B., *Partridge Shooting* (1936) The Sportsman's Library vol. XVII, Philip Allen, London

The Game Conservancy, *Red-legged Partridge*, Booklet No. 18 (1983)

———, *The Grey Partridge*, Booklet No. 4 (1986)

Howard and Moore, *A Complete Checklist of the Birds of the World* (1980) Oxford University Press, London

Johns Revd C. A., F.L.S., *British Game Birds and their Haunts* (1861) 25th edn. Edited by W. B. Alexander M.A., M.B.O.U. Routledge and Kegan Paul Ltd, London

'Marksman', *The Dead Shot* (1860) Longman, Green, Longman, and Roberts, London

O'Connor Raymond J. and Michael Shrubb, *Farming and Birds* (1986) Cambridge University Press, Cambridge

Sedgwick Noel M., *The Young Shot* (1940) Adam and Charles Black, London

Shooting Notes and Comments (1910) Kynoch Ltd, Birmingham

Standfield F. G., *Syndicate Shooting* (1961) Herbert Jenkins, London

Vesey-FitzGerald Brian F.L.S., *The New Naturalist, British Game* (1946) Collins, St James Place, London

White Gilbert, *The Natural History of Selborne* (1962) The Folio Society Ltd

APPENDIX

Partridge are included in the Order of birds called Galliformes. That Order includes birds such as the domestic fowl and the birds which comprise it are well adapted to walking and to a vegetable diet. Within that Order of birds is the family known as the Phasianidae which consist of 183 species, basically, as the name implies, of the pheasant type. It includes a number of genera, or kinds or sub-divisions if you like, of partridge. Each of these genera consists of one or more species and each species may have one or more sub-species. The genera with which we are concerned are *Alectoris*, which includes the Red-leg (*Alectoris rufa*) and *Perdix* which includes the Grey (*Perdix Perdix*)

The species comprising each of these genera are as follows:

Alectoris graeca	Rock Partridge
Alectoris chukar	Chukar Partridge
Alectoris magna	Przewalski Rock Partridge
Alectoris philbyi	Philby's Rock Partridge
Alectoris barbara	Barbary Partridge
Alectoris rufa	Red-legged Partridge
Alectoris melanocephala	Arabian Chukar Partridge

and

Perdix perdix	Grey Partridge
Perdix dauricae	Daurian Partridge
Perdix hodgsoniae	Tibetan Partridge

From the *Alectoris* genus I give the sub-species of *Alectoris rufa*, of *Alectoris graeca* (the Rock Partridge) and *Alectoris chukar* (the Chukar) because these are the birds I suspect of being in one way or another responsible for the Ogridge. From *Perdix* I give the sub-species for *Perdix perdix* (the Grey). For these details from the family Phasianide I am indebted to the work, *A Complete Checklist of the Birds of the World* by Richard Howard and Alick Moore.

Appendix

Red-legged Partridge	*Alectoris rufa*
Sub-species	
A.r. *rufa*	S.C. Europe
A.r. *hispanica*	N.W. Spain and N. Portugal
A.r. *intercedens*	S. Spain
A.r. *corsa*	Corsica
A.r. *australis*	Gran Canaria Is.
Rock Partridge	*Alectoris graeca*
A.g. *saxatilis*	Alps
A.g. *graeca*	S.E. Europe
A.g. *scotti*	Crete
A.g. *sinaica*	Syria to Sinai
A.g. *daghestanica*	N. Caucasus
A.g. *caucasica*	S. Caucasus
A.g. *werae*	S.W. Iran
A.g. *koroviakovi*	E. and S. Iran
A.g. *shestoperovi*	S. Transcaspia
A.g. *subpallida*	Kyzylkum Mts
A.g. *falki*	W. and C. Tien Shan Mts
A.g. *dzungarica*	Tarbagatai Mts
A.g. *fallax*	E. Tien Shan Mts
A.g. *pallida*	S. Chinese Turkestan
A.g. *pallescens*	N. India
A.g. *obscurata*	W. Tannu Ola Mts
Chukar Partridge	*Alectoris chukar*
A.c. *kleini*	E. Greece
A.c. *cypriotes*	Cyclades, Asia Minor
A.c. *kurdestanica*	S. Kurdistan
A.c. *chukar*	Himalayas
A.c. *potanini*	W. Mongolia
A.c. *pubescens*	S. Manchuria, N. China
Grey Partridge	*Perdix perdix*
P.p. *perdix*	British Isles, W. and C. Europe
P.p. *armoricana*	N.W. France
P.p. *sphagnetorum*	N.E. Holland, N.W. Germany
P.p. *hispaniensis*	Pyrenees, N. Spain
P.p. *italica*	Italy
P.p. *lucida*	N.E. Europe
P.p. *robusta*	N.W. Russia
P.p. *arenicola*	W.C. Russia
P.p. *furvescens*	S.W. Russia, N. Iran
P.p. *canescens*	Transcaucasia to N.W. Iran